VOLUME 9

D1559282

JUL 2003

RSAC 3

JOB

Gregory M. Weeks

ABINGDON PRESS
Nashville

JOB

This book is printed on recycled, acid-free paper.

Library of Congress Cataloging-in-Publication Data
Cokesbury basic Bible commentary.
    Bible commentary/by Linda B. Hinton . . . [et al.].
        p.   cm.
    Originally published: Cokesbury basic Bible commentary. Nashville
Graded Press © 1988.
    ISBN 0-687-02620-2 (pbk.: v. 1: alk. paper)
    1. Bible—Commentaries.   I. Hinton, Linda B.   II. Title.
[BS491.2.C65   1994]
220.7—dc20   94-10965
                                                                              CIP

ISBN 0-687-02628-8 (v. 9, Job)
ISBN 0-687-02620-2 (v. 1, Genesis)
ISBN 0-687-02621-0 (v. 2, Exodus–Leviticus)
ISBN 0-687-02622-9 (v. 3, Numbers–Deuteronomy)
ISBN 0-687-02623-7 (v. 4, Joshua–Ruth)
ISBN 0-687-02624-5 (v. 5, 1–2 Samuel)
ISBN 0-687-02625-3 (v. 6, 1–2 Kings)
ISBN 0-687-02626-1 (v. 7, 1–2 Chronicles)
ISBN 0-687-02627-X (v. 8, Ezra–Esther)
ISBN 0-687-02629-6 (v. 10, Psalms)
ISBN 0-687-02630-X (v. 11, Proverbs–Song of Solomon)
ISBN 0-687-02631-8 (v. 12, Isaiah)
ISBN 0-687-02632-6 (v. 13, Jeremiah–Lamentations)
ISBN 0-687-02633-4 (v. 14, Ezekiel–Daniel)
ISBN 0-687-02634-2 (v. 15, Hosea–Jonah)
ISBN 0-687-02635-0 (v. 16, Micah–Malachi)
ISBN 0-687-02636-9 (v. 17, Matthew)
ISBN 0-687-02637-7 (v. 18, Mark)
ISBN 0-687-02638-5 (v. 19, Luke)
ISBN 0-687-02639-3 (v. 20, John)
ISBN 0-687-02640-7 (v. 21, Acts)
ISBN 0-687-02642-3 (v. 22, Romans)
ISBN 0-687-02643-1 (v. 23, 1–2 Corinthians)
ISBN 0-687-02644-X (v. 24, Galatians–Ephesians)
ISBN 0-687-02645-8 (v. 25, Philippians–2 Thessalonians)
ISBN 0-687-02646-6 (v. 26, 1 Timothy–Philemon)
ISBN 0-687-02647-4 (v. 27, Hebrews)
ISBN 0-687-02648-2 (v. 28, James–Jude)
ISBN 0-687-02649-0 (v. 29, Revelation)
ISBN 0-687-02650-4 (complete set of 29 vols.)

99 00 01 02 03—10 9 8 7 6 5 4 3 2

MANUFACTURED IN THE UNITED STATES OF AMERICA

Contents

Outline of Job

I. Prose Introduction (1:1-2:13)
   A. Job's prosperity (1:1-5)
   B. The testing of Job (1:6-2:10)
      1. The first series of hardships (1:6-22)
         a. Destruction of property and family (1:6-19)
         b. Job's refusal to sin (1:20-22)
      2. The second series of hardships (2:1-10)
         a. Affliction of sores (2:1-8)
         b. Job's refusal to sin (2:9-10)
   C. Introduction of Job's friends (2:11-13)
II. Job's Cursing of His Life (3:1-26)
III. Job's Dialogue with His Three Friends (4:1-27:23)
   A. The first series of conversations (4:1-14:22)
      1. Eliphaz's speech (4:1-5:27)
      2. Job's response to Eliphaz (6:1-7:21)
      3. Bildad's speech (8:1-25)
      4. Job's response to Bildad (9:1-10:22)
      5. Zophar's speech (11:1-20)
      6. Job's response to Zophar (12:1-14:22)
   B. The second series of conversations (15:1-21:34)
      1. Eliphaz's speech (15:1-35)
      2. Job's response to Eliphaz (16:1-17:16)
      3. Bildad's speech (18:1-21)
      4. Job's response to Bildad (19:1-29)
      5. Zophar's speech (20:1-29)
      6. Job's response to Zophar (21:1-34)
   C. The third series of conversations (22:1-27:23)
      1. Eliphaz's speech (22:1-30)
      2. Job's response to Eliphaz (23:1-24:17)
      3. Friend's fragment (24:18-25)
      4. Bildad's speech fragment (25:1-6)
      5. Job's response to Bildad fragment (26:1-4)

Introduction to Job

The moment you open the book of Job, you enter a mysterious world. Strange words and phrases bombard your senses. A shady character named Satan challenges God. An old man curses his sores and calls the Lord a variety of ancient names. When God speaks, it's not in any manner we recognize. The divine voice is heard over the roar of a whirling dust storm.

In spite of this alien nature—or perhaps because of it—the book of Job has a magnetic quality. When Rabbi Kushner wrote his best-selling book *When Bad Things Happen to Good People* a few years ago, he began with an interpretation of Job. In so doing, he continued a millenia-old tradition: When people suffer, they turn to the experiences and wisdom found in this ancient book. In journeying with Job as he wrestles with cruel and unexplainable pain, people encounter God in a new and different way.

This same opportunity is open to us. If God is to speak to us in this manner, though, our eyes must first grow accustomed to the unfamiliar world of Job.

Job: The Man and the Legend

Job was the central character in a popular story circulated in the ancient Middle East (the region around the Mediterranean Sea that included Egypt, the Sinai peninsula, and Canaan). Job was a wealthy man living in Uz, which possibly was the ancient country of Edom, an area east of Palestine in the Syrian desert. He was a semi-tragic figure in that he encountered intense—and undeserved—hardships. He lost possessions and health, and became a social outcast. Throughout these sufferings, brought on as a result of a heavenly dispute, Job did not "curse God." In the end, consequently, his possessions, health, and status were restored.

The biblical writers were well acquainted with this story. References to Job were made by Ezekiel (14:14, 20) and James (5:11).

As was the custom in ancient Middle Eastern literature, the name signifies the nature and action of the character. *Job* has been traced to a variety of meanings stemming from both Hebrew and Arabic roots: *one who is at war with God; one born to be persecuted;* and *the repentant one* are possible interpretations.

How the Book Was Written

As Israel lived with its neighbors, it was natural that ideas and experiences of those countries found their way into Israelite culture. The Hebrew sages reflected upon these impressions within the context of their faith in the Lord *(Yahweh)*. The result was the Wisdom Literature found in the Old Testament. This literature is philosophical, with an emphasis upon teaching: Ecclesiastes, Proverbs, several psalms (1, 34, and 92, for example), and parts of other books.

Job is included in this wisdom tradition. In the early sixth century B.C. the Babylonians enslaved the citizens of Judah and deported the useful ones to Babylon. This period of biblical history, known as the *Exile*, was traumatic, causing a crisis of faith for those who believed in God's providential care.

It was against this historical backdrop that the book of Job was written. A wise man/poet of Judah found the

8

ancient legend to be an appropriate vehicle by which to examine faith in God in light of the national catastrophe. The tale he appropriated and edited may be found in the prose portions at the beginning and the end of the book (1:1-2:13; 42:7-17). The first part describes Job's sufferings and his virtuous character, while the last portion depicts the restoration of Job's fortunes. The poetic section in between reveals the poet's painful crisis of faith.

The exception to this is the section containing Elihu's speeches. These chapters (32:1-37:24) are viewed by many scholars as being foreign to the original poem. They were probably penned by a later hand.

The Theme of the Book

It is popular to say that the central thrust of the book of Job is dealing with the question, "Why do the righteous suffer if there is a loving God?" This is actually, however, a sub-theme. The major motif instead is the larger question, "What is the nature of faith—how are we to relate to God?"

The poet verbalizes, through the mouths of Job's friends, the popular theology of ancient Israel. Put simply, this theology is: Do good, and God will reward you; do evil, and God will punish you. This is the idea of *divine retribution.*

Job's replies to his friends, on the other hand, refute this simplistic theology. He stubbornly maintains his righteousness, asserting that his suffering cannot be based on anything he did. If Job is correct, then the theology of his friends—and of the ancient Hebrews, somewhat—has become bankrupt.

Stripped of such an easy view of faith and the world, how, then, can one approach God? This theme is a reflection of the times in which the poet wrote. The nation was in shambles. The old principles and certainties had been turned upside down. Through the words of Job the poet searches for a faith that will discover God in the midst of fear and chaos.

The Structure and Text of Job

The bulk of the poetry section—the part sandwiched between the prose beginning and ending—consists of the dialogue between Job and three "friends" who come to console him: Eliphaz, Bildad, and Zophar. The conversation follows a set form: Eliphaz speaks, Job replies; Bildad speaks, Job replies; Zophar speaks, Job replies.

This forms a cycle of speeches, and there are three such cycles. (The third cycle, 22:1-27:23, is not complete, containing only the speeches of Eliphaz and Bildad, along with Job's replies.) Preceding and following this series of speeches, Job gives a pair of eloquent soliloquies regarding his suffering (3; 29:1-31:40). A fourth friend, Elihu, follows Job's last soliloquy. Instead of conversing with Job, he makes a long series of speeches (32:6-37:24).

The poetry section concludes with the dialogue between God and Job. God makes two speeches, with Job responding to each. With this conversation the conflict is resolved, leading to the prose conclusion.

The Hebrew text of this poetry section is very poor in places. As can be seen in the footnotes in the NRSV, translators in many instances had to make educated guesses regarding the meaning of a word or phrase. In addition, the third cycle of conversation between Job and his friends appears abrupt and illogical in places. This cycle contains fragments of other speeches; see the commentary on this section.

Types of Literature Found in Job

Just as an epic novel may use different types of literature (adventure, romance, mystery), so does the author of Job. The poet, standing in the Hebrew wisdom tradition, employed different literary forms that were well recognized by his audience.

The first, and most obvious, was that of the *narrative*. In the prose sections the author adapted the ancient story of Job. This storytelling style was the basic vehicle by which God's interaction with the Hebrew people was transmitted.

The poem itself has the characteristics of a *legal document*. The dialogue between Job and his friends has the flavor of a debate. In addition, Job often appeals for a judge to decide between himself and the one who is responsible for his unjust treatment—God (9:33). Finally, with the debate with his friends ended, Job calls for God to enter the courtroom and state the divine case against him.

The third major type of literature employed was the *lament*. Several of the psalms (such as 22, 39, 77, 88, 102) employ this form, wherein a sufferer expresses powerful emotions to God and cries out for help. The poet used this throughout his work, most poignantly in Job's two soliloquies.

A Hint on Reading the Book of Job

To enter Job's world is to enter an environment alien to us. Consequently, while it is important to get a clear understanding of a passage, at times this is impossible. Ancient ways of looking at the world, corruptions in the text of Job, and uncertain Hebrew words and phrases assure us of this.

Using another instrument—your own experience—will help you deal with such a limitation. Read Job with one eye on his world and another on your own world. Read the book with an understanding of your own pain and the pain of those around you. Ask yourself if the words you find on Job's lips or on his friends' have ever been on your own.

The gap between Job's world and ours—made by the centuries that have passed since the poet first scratched on parchment—is enormous. Reading the book with your own experiences just under the surface will help bridge that gap. By doing this you will share the poet's wrestling with the Lord, and his ultimate victory will be yours as well.

PART ONE

Job 1–2

Introduction to These Chapters

These two prose chapters dramatically set the stage for the rest of the book. Presenting Job's "rise and fall," they contain the first part of the ancient legend of the righteous sufferer (see Introduction, "How the Book Was Written"). The poet relates the legend up to the point where Job silently sits in the ashes with his friends (2:13). This provides the springboard from which the poet launches into his theological reflections. It is not until the latter verses of chapter 42 that he picks up the tale again, bringing the book to a conclusion.

As in a movie dramatizing a fable from Greek or Roman mythology, the action alternates between earthly and heavenly arenas. No sooner is Job introduced than the scene switches to an other-worldly palace. There God enters into a heated exchange with Satan, the end result being a wager as to whether or not Job fears God *for nothing* (1:9). After two sets of trials, Job has not cursed God (2:5, 9), and it appears as if the Almighty has won.

Such drama seems alien not only to us, but it is also foreign to the rest of the Old Testament. Nowhere else can be found such detailed heavenly theatrics. The crux of our uneasiness lies in the affront to our theological sensitivity. Can God lose control and be influenced by Satan? Does God allow intense suffering, just to settle a bet? How does this square with our belief in a compassionate, just God?

When we ask ourselves such questions, we must remember that the story of Job was drawn not from Israel but from other lands in the ancient Middle East, countries that did not share the Hebrew faith. The legend was entrenched in the religion of these nations, a religion that included the belief in several gods. The strongest of these deities ruled, and a heavenly "palace" scene, with the great god reviewing the others and losing his temper, was very believable. The Hebrew poet, following the Wisdom style (see Introduction, "How the Book Was Written"), screened the story through his eyes of faith. Nonetheless, the sense of the unusual remains in reading these chapters.

Perhaps the best we can do in reading these chapters is to remember the author's purpose. These verses are introductory. Although we may gain some theological insights, they should not be pressed. The Hebrew writer, in breathtaking fashion, has simply prepared us for the real theological issue: the relationship between God and a suffering humanity.

Here is an outline of chapters 1–2.
 I. Job's Prosperity and Righteousness (1:1-5)
 II. The Testing of Job (1:6-2:10)
   A. The first series of hardships (1:6-22)
   B. The second series of hardships (2:1-10)
 III. The Introduction of Job's Friends (2:11-13)

Job's Prosperity and Righteousness (1:1-5)

The author establishes two unshakable facts in this brief passage. The most important is in the first verse: Job was blameless and upright. So conscientious was he that he painstakingly offered sacrifices to God, in case he or his children sinned (verse 5). The second fact stemmed from this righteousness. Job was rewarded with great wealth (verses 2-3).

Uz (verse 1) was an area east of Palestine, in the Syrian desert. It was possibly the ancient name for Edom.

East (verse 3) refers to the countries east of Palestine, such as Uz. This area was known for its scholars (see Matthew 2:1).

The First Series of Hardships (1:6-22)

The section begins with the making of the wager between God and Satan. In this contest as to whether or not Job is holy because of God's blessings, there is only one rule to be observed: Job's health is off-limits to Satan.

The catastrophes cascade over the old man in rapid succession. No sooner does one messenger convey bad news than another arrives *(while he was still speaking, another came,* verses 16-18). The worst calamities of all were the deaths of his ten children; verse 13 foreshadows this last event, described in verses 18-19.

Sons of God (verse 6 Hebrew; NIV, *angels,* NRSV, *heavenly beings*) was an ancient term for divine beings, or angels (see Psalms 29:1; 82:6; 89:6). They are appearing before a heavenly court presided over by God.

Satan (verse 6) does not carry the evil connotations associated with the term in the New Testament. In Hebrew it means simply *the adversary,* one who opposes. Thus, the term is not a proper name but rather a description of one of the sons of God (see Numbers 22:22). This figure is like a prosecuting attorney, challenging God's claim of Job's purity.

Sabeans (verse 15) were inhabitants of a region in the southern section of the Arabian peninsula, an area south of Job's country.

Chaldeans (verse 17) were inhabitants of a rugged region in southern Babylonia. Babylonia was north of Uz. The marauders, thus, descended upon Job from all sides—the Sabeans from the south and the Chaldeans from the north.

Tore his robe and shaved his head (verse 20) signified acts of mourning.

The LORD (verse 21) was an intimate term for God,

suggestive of a special covenantal relationship. It stems from Exodus 4:11, where the name of God is revealed to Moses as *Yahweh* and translated throughout the Old Testament as LORD. Job's use of the term in verse 21 suggests his closeness to God as well as his continued righteousness.

The Second Series of Hardships (2:1-10)

Following Job's successful endurance of the first wave of suffering, another heavenly court scene ensues. God acknowledges being baited by Satan into allowing the test of Job, but proudly points to the suffer's steadfast virtue (verse 3). The Adversary responds that the hardships were not tough enough, so the contest begins again. This time Satan can inflict physical pain.

Verses 1-3 repeat 1:6-8. The only addition is the latter part of verse 3, where God notes Job's endurance.

Skin for skin! (verse 4) is an ancient proverbial phrase, probably used by traders, the precise meaning of which is unknown. The sense of it is found in the remainder of the verse: A person will do anything to save her or his life.

Loathsome sores (verse 7 NRSV; NIV, *painful sores*) are not leprosy, but nonetheless an intense skin disease.

Potsherd (verse 8 NRSV) is a sharp sliver of broken pottery (So NIV).

With the words *curse God and die* (verse 9), Job's wife wishes to shorten his agony. The act of cursing God would bring death.

Shall we accept good from God? (verse 10 NIV). Note that Job does not use the intimate term for God (LORD, 1:21), nor does he offer a blessing.

The Introduction of Job's Friends (2:11-13)

Job's three friends, upon hearing of the "evil" he has encountered, arrange to visit him. This trip would take at least several days, since they live to the north of Uz. They are moved by a genuine concern for him and a desire to console and comfort (verse 11). Their compassion deepens when they do not even recognize him, and they are moved to express their anguish (verse 12).

Eliphaz the Temanite. The oldest of the friends, his name possibly means *God is fine gold.* He is from Tema, a town in the northern Arabian peninsula known for its commerce (see also 6:19).

Bildad the Shuhite. His name has been understood as either *God has loved* or *son of Hadad.* He is from the tribe of Shuah, which possibly settled in the northeastern part of the Arabian peninsula.

Zophar the Naamathite. Possibly meaning *singing bird,* Zophar was from Na'ameh, a region in northwest Arabia.

These three sit with Job *seven days and seven nights* (verse 13), the traditional length of mourning for the dead (see Genesis 50:10; 1 Samuel 31:13). Out of respect they keep silent, waiting for Job to speak.

§ § § § § § §

The Message of Job 1–2

Often, when we find ourselves suffering, we ask, "Is there a purpose behind this pain?" Our assumption is that God has a benevolent plan, either to teach us something or to accomplish a greater good.

These two chapters explode such thinking. Job's suffering being based on a bet makes the thought of a wise plan behind pain ludicrous. Perhaps the author is saying: "Don't look for rhyme or reason behind your pain. It can't be understood!"

Just as the tale of God's wager with Satan undermines such thinking, it also offers a thread of hope for us. In the dialogue with the Adversary, we see God's emotional side. The Lord passionately loves Job; a proud parent's words are found in 1:8 and 2:3. *Have you considered my servant Job? There is none like him on the earth.*

Only a God who can become passionately involved with persons can speak to us in our pain. The Lord's love for Job ultimately produces a whirlwind visitation (chapters 38-41)—a stupendous event, considering the curses Job has hurled against the Almighty in the preceding chapters. And God's passion for us produced an even greater visitation—the life, death, and resurrection of Jesus the Christ.

Connected to this are Job's reactions in these two chapters. As noted in the commentary on 2:10, there is a subtle change in his mood. With continued suffering and the lessening of a hope for an easy way out, Job begins slipping into despair. He is about to embark on a journey that will lead him onto a spiritual cross. His cries—like ours—will strike deep into God's heart. God will leave neither Job nor us hanging there alone.

§ § § § § § §

Job 3

Introduction to This Chapter

If the first two chapters set the stage for the rest of the book, then chapter 3 is the opening scene. For seven days and nights Job and his friends have sat in silence (2:13). Job now breaks the stillness. His words set in motion a series of dialogues that, while exploring the nature of faith, will become surprisingly heated.

What he says here contrasts starkly with his pious utterances in chapter 2. His speech takes the form of a lament (see "Types of Literature Found in Job" in the Introduction). There are no blessings here. Instead, he curses his life, questions the justice of existence, hints at God's hardness, and bemoans his wretchedness.

Such surprising, angry cries allow us to catch a glimpse inside Job. The days and nights of silence have provided him an opportunity to reflect on things. When he speaks, he could do so in the manner of the grieving psalmist, who started with lamenting and ended with praising (see Psalm 77). Judging from his words in chapter 2, this would have been logical. His reflection, however, drives away piety. He begins somewhat reservedly, with a curse upon the day he was born, and ends in total despair. For Job, there will be no easy way out, no lapse into traditional theology. He will be expressing himself uninhibitedly.

In addition to this psychological value of Job's speech, there is also a structural one. Imagine he is speaking in a courtroom. He is the prosecuting attorney. God is the defendant. Job's words in chapter 3 can then be seen as the opening argument for the prosecution. He indirectly asserts that he is suffering far more than he should, hinting that God is the cause (3:23b). He also directly questions God's justice: *Why is light given to those in misery?* (3:20). It is interesting to note that Job ends the conversation with his friends by entering into a monologue much more extensive than this one (see Chapters 29-31). This latter speech is his closing argument, after which he rests his case.

Correspondingly, as will be seen in the following chapters, this first monologue has a dramatic effect upon Job's friends. They turn from being comforters to assuming the duties of "defense lawyers." God's character has been assailed, and they take it upon themselves to rally to the defense. Accusations and arguments increasingly take the place of compassion.

Had Job's speech been a continuation of his earlier piety, then his friends would have remained in sympathy with him. He challenges God's justice, however, and the debate begins.

Two other points should be noted regarding this chapter. First, it is written in poetic verse. Chapter 3 begins the author's original work, a poetic masterpiece that will continue—with the exception of 32:1-5 and of some questionable passages—until the closing verses. In Hebrew, this poetry, as in English verse, follows unmistakable patterns, such as in line length and meter.

Second, the chapter appears to be intact, with the possible exception of verse 16. Many commentators believe it is misplaced, having originally followed verse 11.

Here is an outline of chapter 3.
   I. Cursing the Day of His Birth (3:1-10)
  II. Wishing for an Early Death (3:11-19)
 III. Is Living Better Than Dying? (3:20-23)
  IV. Crying Out in Pain (3:24-26)

Cursing the Day of His Birth (3:1-10)

Satan has suggested that Job will curse God (2:5), and Job's wife encouraged him to do so (2:9). His first words after the period of silence are a curse. However, the curse is not directed at God but rather at the day of his birth (verse 1).

Such cursing was a formal way of expressing great anguish (see Jeremiah 20:14-18 for another example). It followed a certain form. There is first a series of *lets* (verses 3-9), conveying ill wishes. This is followed by a *because* statement (verse 10), conveying the reason for the anger. This form is similar to the modern resolution, which has a series of "whereas" clauses followed by a "therefore."

The prevalent curse Job wishes for is *darkness*. The day of his birth is to be shrouded by it (verses 4-5), while the night is to be blanketed with an even murkier covering (verse 6). This image is indicative throughout the book of a total absence of hope; indeed, darkness is where wickedness and evil reign (30:26; 36:20). Job specifies the evil he places on the night of his birth: non-existence (verse 6b); sadness and emptiness (verse 7); hopelessness (verse 9).

Those . . . Leviathan (verse 8) probably refers to sorcerers/magicians who were skilled in calling up evil or mysterious forces (see 1 Samuel 28:3-14). Leviathan was a mythical dragon that periodically swallowed the sun or moon, causing eclipses. Job, thus, is invoking wizards who were capable of producing darkness. Other references to Leviathan are Psalms 74:14; 104:26; Isaiah 27:1. See the commentary on Chapter 41 for further discussion.

Wishing for an Early Death (3:11-19)

Job leaves the formality of the curse and moves into a slightly more personal expression of pain. His life is so wretched now that he wishes one of two things had happened: that he had died at birth (verses 11-12) or that he had died prematurely in the womb (verse 16). Death would have made him happy, since then he could rest, never having encountered such suffering (verse 13).

The other verses reflect Job's view of death as the "great equalizer," a view consistent with Hebrew thought (see Ecclesiastes 2:12-17). There was no notion of an afterlife as we know it. Rather, all persons—from kings to prisoners—shared the same lot: They rested in Sheol (see the commentary on 7:9). That Job wishes for such a state reflects the intensity of his pain.

Is Living Better than Dying? (3:20-23)

Job here takes a step closer to unleashing his feelings—a step that includes hurling anger at God. Whereas the previous sections contain a formal curse and a death wish, in this passage the sufferer starts questioning the fairness of life. Why continue living if death would be preferable to the pain? Job reflects on this in verses 20-23*a*. He finally, and indirectly, acknowledges that God must be behind such injustice (verse 23*b*). Job is not yet ready, however, to make a full and daring accusation against the Almighty.

By starting to question divine justice, Job is beginning to venture down the road that diverges from that of his friends. The outcome will be Job's eventual, explicit condemnation of the view of divine reward/punishment (see the discussion in "The Theme of the Book" in the Introduction).

The verb translated *hedged in* (verse 23 NIV; NRSV, *fenced in*) also means *thoroughly covered.* God isolates someone, totally cutting off that person from everything else.

Crying Out in Pain (3:24-26)

Having stepped to the brink of blasphemy, Job retreats. He ends his monologue by forcefully airing his agony. The formality that began the chapter cannot restrain the raw emotion that empowers the sufferer.

The verses that result reflect this rawness. Whereas the preceding ones are fairly unambiguous and forthright, these appear more enigmatic, packed with images that are unclear. Job is not speaking rationally; rather, he is speaking out of the bewilderment of his soul.

The first part of verse 24 may also mean *my sighing comes before my bread;* Job takes no joy in eating. The second part of the verse points out his weakness (see Psalm 22:14).

Verse 25 can be taken two ways: (1) Everything Job fears is coming true; or (2) God, whom Job *fears* (see 28:28), is coming upon him.

I have no rest (verse 26) shows how relentless his agony is. Even sleep, which would give him some relief, is taken away from him (see also 7:4).

§ § § § § § §

The Message of Job 3

Lurking just below the surface of these verses is a question that must be addressed: *Is your faith adequate to help you in times of trouble?*

Job, at first, found his faith helping him quite nicely. His belief in God, a belief that had rewarded him in so many ways, was a safe retreat. When everything was first taken from him, he could utter the traditional pronouncement, Blessed be the name of the Lord (1:21).

The cursing and the intensifying anger we find in chapter 3, however, show us that his faith was ultimately inadequate. After seven days and nights of silence, when he waited for God's deliverance and it never came, he gave in to the seething emotions inside him. The lament that came from his mouth was, in the final analysis, a lament over the death of his old theology.

What happens if our pain does not go away? Indeed, what happens if, as in Job's case, it multiplies? It is obvious. Our certainties waver, our fervency wanes. If Job—the *blameless and upright* (1:1)—stumbled, so will we.

The answer to the question posed by this chapter is: In the face of sustained pain, our faith will crumble. Our only hope is that out of the ruins a new faith will arise. Emerging from the other side of intense suffering, it will restore our confidence and enable us to live fully once more.

Job eventually reached such a new plateau: However, as the following chapters witness, it was a long and painful process. We, too, can find new strength, if we are willing to pay the price. The first step is acknowledging the limits of the faith we have today.

§ § § § § § §

Job 4–7

Introduction to These Chapters

This section begins with Eliphaz's response to what Job said in chapter 3. This reply inaugurates the first cycle of dialogues between Job and his comforters (see the outline of the book). In each cycle Eliphaz will converse first with Job, since he is the eldest friend. Conversations between Job and Bildad, then Zophar, will follow.

In chapter 3 Job, though expressing bewilderment and strong anger, restrains himself. He could lash out more vehemently, but he does not. It is as if he were testing the waters with his strong feelings.

Likewise, Eliphaz shows restraint in his first address. He is responding, in chapters 4 and 5, to Job's belief that his suffering is unjust and undeserved. Such a thought is contradictory to the major tenet agreed to by all three friends: God makes the wicked suffer and blesses the righteous with health and peace. Instead of harshly debating the sufferer, however, Eliphaz begins timidly and compassionately: If someone ventures a word with you, will you be offended? (4:2). In addition, throughout his speech the friend never directly accuses Job of wrongdoing, and he ends by painting a happy picture of what Job might eventually enjoy.

Such courtesies cannot conceal Eliphaz's disagreement with Job's sentiments, however. The friend is concerned with doing two things in this speech. First, he defends the traditional belief of suffering being the punishment of a just God. He does this by offering what he believes to be certain undeniable theological facts. Second, to support these truths, he wants Job to recognize the authority by which he speaks: divine revelation (4:12-21) and experience/reason (4:8*a*; 5:27).

Job's response is predictable. He feels that his friends will argue and not console. This serves to deepen both his anger and his despair. He begins by doing something he was afraid to do in his earlier lament: directly blaming God (6:4). His anger then swells, first against his friends, then against his own life. Finally, he turns back to God, lashing out against the divine injustice.

In these chapters, then, we witness Job's worst fears being realized. His last hope of support—the three men who are with him when everyone else has fled—is shaken. It appears that they are not going to accept Job as he is, but will try to change him. Faced with this realization, Job now confronts an existence deprived of even the faintest flicker of light. Job is alone.

Turning to critical considerations, these chapters are well preserved. There are a few verses containing Hebrew words of questionable meaning. Other than these, there are no major problems.

Here is an outline of chapters 4-7.
- I. Eliphaz's First Speech (4:1-5:27)
  - A. Courteous introduction (4:1-6)
  - B. The wicked suffer (4:7-11)
  - C. God's purity shows our impurity (4:12-21)
  - D. God does not help the wicked (5:1-16)
  - E. Be humble and trust God (5:17-27)
- II. Job's Reply (6:1-7:21)
  - A. Anger at God (6:1-13)
  - B. Anger at his friends (6:14-30)
  - C. Despair over his life (7:1-6)
  - D. A blasphemous "prayer" (7:7-21)

Courteous Introduction (4:1-6)

The courtesies found in these verses are a rarity. They will quickly disappear in the following chapters as the debate grows more heated. Eliphaz begins humbly (verse 2) and compliments Job profusely (verses 3-4, 6). He believes that with a gentle nudge Job will see things differently, and repent.

Eliphaz praises Job's righteous past in verses 2-4. Eventually, the friend's anger will make him forget this (see 22:2-9).

Fear of God (verse 6 NRSV; NIV = *piety*), or respecting and humbling oneself before the Almighty, is a central concept in the Book of Job (see 28:28). Eliphaz praises Job's fearing God, but in his next two speeches will condemn him for forsaking this (see 15:4; 22:4).

The Wicked Suffer (4:7-11)

Eliphaz refutes Job's claim that his suffering is unjust. It is obvious to all that suffering comes from God in order to punish the wicked (verse 8).

Eliphaz uses the image of the *lion* (verses 10-11) to symbolize the wicked, since a lion preys on the weak and defenseless. A parallel is found in Psalm 58:6.

God's Purity Shows Our Impurity (4:12-21)

Behind Job's belief in divine injustice is his belief in his own righteousness. Eliphaz challenges this by asserting that, compared to a supremely holy God, no mortal can claim purity. So important is this point that Eliphaz claims it was revealed to him directly by God through a dream/vision he had at night (see also 33:14-15, and Numbers 12:6-8 for another example of revelation through visions of the night).

Spirit (verses 15-16) also means, in Hebrew, *breath;* it is the same term used in verse 9. Eliphaz experienced the spirit as a blast of wind that stirred him.

A better rendering of verse 19c is, *who are crushed like the moth.*

As a *tent* collapses when its *cords* are pulled up (verse 21), so does a wicked person topple when God punishes. *Wisdom* refers to the understanding of God's ways, and the appropriate human response (fear of God).

God Does Not Help the Wicked (5:1-16)

Perhaps moved by his preceding reflections, Eliphaz indirectly implies that Job could be numbered among the *fools.* The thought is simple: There is no divine help for Job (verse 1), which is a result of his sinfulness. The tone is still restrained, however.

Holy ones (verse 1b) refers to divine beings, or angels; they are also called the *sons of God* in 1:6 and 2:1.

Verse 2 is proverbial. *Fool* is a term found in Wisdom Literature to denote one who does not fear God.

Verse 4 may be a veiled reference to the deaths of Job's children. The friends do not hesitate mentioning this tragedy as they attempt to persuade Job (see 8:4).

The meaning of verse 5 is difficult. A person who eats *out of thorns* (NRSV; NIV, *among thorns*) is an outcast wandering the wilderness in search of food (see 30:3-7).

Verse 7 is an ancient proverb, like verse 2.

Even the most courteous of Job's friends is amazingly arrogant. Eliphaz has no difficulty in saying what he would do if he were in Job's sandals (verse 8).

Verses 9-16 form a doxology, praising God's punishing the wicked and blessing the weak. This God will help Job if the sufferer repents.

Be Humble and Trust God (5:17-27)

Having described God's just nature, Eliphaz now elaborates upon the joys Job will enjoy if he stops claiming that his suffering is unfair. Things appear simple to Eliphaz. Job has only to admit his sin, and his torment will end.

The thought of suffering being beneficial to the sufferer is elaborated upon in detail by Elihu in verses 17-18 (see chapters 36-37).

From six calamities (NIV; NRSV, *troubles*); *in seven . . .* (verse 19) is an ancient literary way of saying *several times*. It is not meant to be taken literally.

The phrase, *stones of the field* (verse 23), is difficult to understand. Some have thought the poet originally meant "field spirits," demon-like creatures responsible for the dangers that may befall a person in the wilderness. Such beings were part of the religion of countries neighboring Judah. The sense of the verse, anyway, is that Job will have nothing to fear wherever he goes.

Verse 27 indicates that the friends are in agreement with each other, standing united against Job.

Anger at God (6:1-13)

Not hearing any help from Eliphaz, Job despairingly plunges ahead. He ended chapter 3 hinting that God hedged him in (3:23). Now he bluntly charges that God, like a skilled archer, has cruelly made him the target of *the arrows of the Almighty* (6:4).

Rash (verse 3 NRSV; NIV *impetuous*) is not apologetic; rather, it carries here the sense of *wild* and *raving*.

The term for *terrors* (verse 4) is used in Psalm 88:15; there, as well as here, it conveys the feeling of a wounded victim as a killer approaches to finish the job.

Verse 5 is proverbial. Only when a creature is in need—or pain—does it cry out.

Purslane (verse 6 NIV, *the white of an egg*; NRSV, *the juice of mallows*) was a small, weed-like plant that had a bland juice. It was used in salads.

Job's death, in addition to alleviating his pain, would vindicate him. God would be killing one who had not *denied the words of the Holy One* (verse 10). The Almighty, then, would be seen as the sinful one.

In the previous chapters Eliphaz had encouraged Job to endure patiently God's chastening (5:17). Job responds by saying he has neither the strength nor the reason to do this (verse 11).

Anger at His Friends (6:14-30)

Just as God will not help Job, neither will his friends. This realization causes the sufferer to vent his frustration directly at them.

In verses 15-20, Job compares his friends to temporary desert streams. *Caravans* will seek them, only to find them dried up.

A *torrent-bed* (verse 15 NRSV; NIV, *intermittent streams*) is a swift, dangerous stream carrying a strong current. *Freshets* (NRSV) are temporary streams (so NIV) of water resulting from melting ice or snow.

Tema (verse 19) is the residence of Eliphaz, known for its commerce (see commentary on 2:11-13). *Sheba* is another name for the home of the Sabaeans, the marauders who stole Job's cattle and killed his servants (see 1:15).

Job is not seeking anything costly from his friends (verses 21c-23), so they should not be *afraid*. He only wants their compassionate understanding.

In verses 24-26, Job asks his friends to be specific in their advice to him. He doesn't want simply to be criticized.

Turn (verse 29 NRSV; NIV, *Relent*) may be a reference to Job's friends turning away from him in response to his caustic critique of them. They may be on the verge of leaving. Job is begging them to stay. He still recognizes his need for human company.

Despair Over His Life (7:1-6)

Feeling the wrath of both friends and God, Job again laments his existence.

A *hired man* (verse 1 NIV; NRSV, *laborer*), or servant, led a life of hard work and little freedom.

The only relief a *slave* (verse 2) may receive toiling under the hot sun is a brief rest in the shade (*shadow*).

Months in verse 3 may refer to a term of service of an indentured servant, such as Jacob's indenture to Laban for seven years (Genesis 29:18). The length of Job's suffering is never specified, though several months seems unlikely.

In a healthy life, the night should be short and peaceful while the day should be long and prosperous (verses 4-6). The opposite is true in Job's case: The nights are long, providing no relief, and the days are short and meaningless.

The *weaver's shuttle* (verse 6) is the part of a loom that passes rapidly back and forth, weaving yarn into cloth.

A Blasphemous "Prayer" (7:7-21)

Job turns desperately to God. He reverts to the traditional pious plea, *Remember . . .* , found in many of the psalmists' prayers (see Psalms 25:7; 74:2; 78:39). He cannot continue in this vein, however; God's abandonment has hurt him deeply. This feeling gives rise to the *therefore* (verse 11), after which his prayer turns to addressing God with unrestrained *bitterness*.

In ancient Hebrew thought, *Sheol* (verse 9 NRSV; NIV, *the grave*) was the realm of the dead, located under the earth. Not to be confused with the New Testament concept of "Hell," this was simply a murky resting place, viewed neither as reward nor punishment. This is not God's domain; the dead are not remembered (see 7:21b).

The *sea* and the *monster of the deep* (verse 12 NIV; NRSV, *Dragon*) represent the chaos God had to subdue in order for Creation to take place (see the commentary on 3:8 and on chapter 41). This verse is ironical: If Job is not guarded by God, will he endanger all creation?

Verse 14: Instead of the divine revelations Eliphaz enjoys (4:13-16), Job has only terrible nightmares.

Verse 17 is a parody of Psalms 8:4 and 144:3-4.

Verse 19 is the ancient equivalent of, "I can't even catch my breath!"

Verses 20-21: Job is not admitting any guilt. He is, instead, agreeing with Eliphaz (4:12-21) that God is all-powerful and all-holy. If that is the case, why is God so viciously affected by human transgression? Why does the Almighty react to sinners so violently? Note that *target* refers to Job being the target of God's *arrows* (6:4a)

Verse 21*b* is a bitter conclusion. When God eventually has a change of heart and wants a relationship with Job as it was in the past (see 29:1-6), it will be too late. The sufferer will have descended to Sheol.

§ § § § § § §

The Message of Job 4–7

These chapters carry further the message of chapter 3. There we saw that in the face of sustained pain, our faith sill crumble. Here the poet makes it more specific. As if to make sure we do not miss this point, he shows us that in the face of sustained pain, we will abandon our old way of praying.

Eliphaz does nothing more than reinforce the theology that is now meaningless to Job. The sufferer at first reacts angrily. Then, in chapter 7, he makes a last-ditch effort to regain his sanity. Humbly he begins a prayer (7:7). No sooner are the traditional words out of his mouth, however, than he abandons the attempt (7:11). They sound as hollow to him as the theology Eliphaz preaches—the theology Job once believed.

When we are at a crisis in our faith due to suffering, how do we pray? We first start, like Job, with the familiar. Perhaps we recite prayers we've memorized, such as the Lord's Prayer. Maybe we begin with comfortable phrases such as, "Dear Lord, please help me . . . " But how long does our tradition sustain us?

When our tradition disintegrates, we start praying in a different language. Instead of praising and beseeching, our prayers are filled with accusing. Why isn't God helping us?

Paradoxically, talking to God in this way is the ultimate expression of faith. It takes seriously the covenantal relationship we have with our Creator. When we honestly expose ourselves, we trust that God can hear us and then act for us.

§ § § § § § §

Job 8–10

Introduction to These Chapters

Eliphaz's speech (chapters 4–5) laid the foundation for the remaining discourses of the friends. In a sense, it serves as an overview of what we will hear them telling Job. All three will defend God's reputation of being just. They will do this by citing the suffering of the wicked and the prosperity of the blameless, the focal point of the traditional theology they espouse. These men are not clones of each other, though. The quirks of their individual personalities distinguish them. Contrasting Bildad and Eliphaz is a good example.

In chapter 8 Bildad makes his appearance. His discourse starkly contrasts with that of Eliphaz in both style and tone. The elder friend began courteously (4:2), then gently built his argument to the point where he thought Job could be nudged into repenting (5:27). Bildad dispenses with such civilities. He chastises and attempts to scare Job in his introduction, a six-verse "sermon." He then bullies Job by appealing to tradition (verses 8-10), before finally painting the traditional picture of the wicked's destruction. Instead of being a kindly teacher, he embodies a fiery preacher.

Unintentionally, these first two friends have become the classic police interrogation team. One is "nice" while the other is "mean." Bildad's white-hot anger at the sufferer's refusal to change allows him to assume such a role. His rage is so intense that he can only blurt out a few sentences before he must sit down: Eliphaz's speech covered two chapters while Bildad's fills only one.

Job's response to such fire and brimstone is easy to guess. If Eliphaz's tenderness did not quell the sufferer's rage at the Almighty, Bildad's bluntness will only serve to intensify it. Thus far Job has claimed that God is unjust solely in dealing with him. He has made accusations of being selected as God's target (7:20). In light of Bildad's harangue, Job takes yet another step toward blasphemy: God is not only unjust to him, but allows the wicked to control the earth (9:24). Job waves yet another red flag in front of his comforters.

Job prefaces this outburst, however, by making a profound theological point. Eliphaz had said that God's righteousness makes all people, by comparison, sinful (4:17). Job begins his address by drawing the logical conclusion: *How can a mortal be righteous* (NIV; NRSV, *just before God?* (9:2) Since people have no claim whatsoever upon God, then humanity is at the Almighty's mercy. This realization will serve as the basis for a repeated plea throughout the book for an *umpire* (9:33) that will hold the divine power in check.

Critically speaking, these chapters are well preserved. Apart from the customary difficult and sometimes obscure verses scattered throughout, this section appears to be complete.

Here is an outline of chapters 8–10:
I. Bildad's First Speech (8:1-22)
   A. Chastisement of Job (8:1-2)
   B. God's justice regarding Job (8:3-7)
   C. God's punishment of the wicked (8:8-19)
   D. Job's only hope (8:20-22)
II. Job's Reply (9:1–10:22)
   A. God's overwhelming power (9:1-10)
   B. God's consequent injustice (9:11-35)
   C. Job's accusatory prayer (10:1-22)

Chastisement of Job (8:1-12)

The preacher has no time for niceties. He begins his speech with an angry impatience. He sees things so clearly that he is indignant at Job's hesitancies. Why doesn't Job just repent?

Consistent with his impatience, Bildad uses his opening phrase, *How long,* to begin his second speech (18:2). *A great wind* (NRSV; NIV, *blustering wind*) may also be translated, *a great storm.* He is belittling Job's thoughts and feelings.

God's Justice Regarding Job (8:3-7)

Bildad offers a statement he thinks is obvious, without need of proof: God cannot *pervert* justice (verse 3). To illustrate this, and to intimidate, he mentions how the deaths of Job's children were a result of their sin. This friend displays no sensitivity whatsoever.

Verse 7: If Job repents, then his future will be even greater than his past. The irony is that Job's wealth will be restored double (see 42:12-15), but not because he succumbs to the traditional theology of the friends.

God's Punishment of the Wicked (8:8-19)

The remainder of Bildad's speech is composed mostly of his painting the conventional picture of the wicked person's fate. Whereas Eliphaz appealed to divine revelation as proof of his theology, Bildad looks to what the ancestors have learned (verse 8).

Bildad quotes a proverb in verse 11, perhaps Egyptian (*papyrus* grows profusely in the Nile). In light of his preceding appeal to tradition, it is appropriate that he uses here a well-known ancient saying. Papyrus and other *reeds* are fragile plants which can easily be destroyed—just as the wicked can be (verses 12-13).

Compare verses 16-17 to Matthew 13:5-6, a part of Jesus' parable of the sower.

It will deny him (verse 18 NRSV; NIV; *disown*) refers to

the dwelling of the wicked person. When a sinner is punished by God, there will be absolutely nothing left.

Verse 19 is meant sarcastically. *Out of the earth others will spring* means that, like the papyrus, the wicked will continue to bloom and die.

Job's Only Hope (8:20-22)

If Job repents (see 8:5) and becomes blameless (verse 20; see also 8:6), then he will be saved. Once again, the solution to Job's suffering is simple in Bildad's eyes.

Like verse 7, the poet may intend irony in verse 22. By *those who hate you* (NRSV; NIV *your enemies*) *will be clothed in shame,* the author may be subtly referring to Job's friends. As seen in 42:7-9, these three comforters will eventually have to implore Job's prayers. The poet thus adds a comic touch to the blustery Bildad.

God's Overwhelming Power (9:1-10)

Job immediately attacks the soft underbelly of his friends' theology. No matter how good or bad a person is, that person is still at the mercy of an all-powerful and—to Job—capricious God. *How can a mortal be just before God?* (verse 2b). The remaining verses in the section describe the divine power, a strength that crushes humanity.

Verse 3: If one wished to contend (NRSV; NIV, *dispute*) *with him.* This is Job's desire. His reflection on his inability to do this leads to his wish for an *umpire* (9:33).

Verse 4: Wise in heart (NRSV; NIV, *His wisdom is profound*). The heart was believed to be the center of intellectual activity, in contrast to our view of it being the seat of the emotions. (See Proverbs 24:12 and Jeremiah 4:19.)

Verses 6-9: God's power as Creator is a prevalent theme in the latter part of the book; see the similar images and phrases in 26:8-11 and 38:31-33. The *Bear* refers to constellations of stars containing either the Big

Dipper ("Great Bear") or the Little Dipper ("Little Bear").
Orion is a constellation of stars representing the famous
hunter in Greek mythology. The *Pleiades* is a cluster of
stars located in the constellation Taurus. *Chambers*
(NRSV; NIV *constellations*) *of the South* refers to a group of
stars whose location is unidentifiable.

Note the Revised Standard Version's alternate reading
of verse 8b: trampled the *naves of the sea*. This refers to the
subduing of Leviathan (see verse 13).

God's Consequent Injustice (9:11-35)

This section is one of the bitterest found in the Bible.
The powerful Creator does not relate to Job lovingly, but
rather as a thief (verses 11-12). Moreover, this God is also
a liar. If Job could bring the deity to trial, God would
pervert whatever Job could say (*I am blameless*, verse 20).
The sufferer generalizes from this that God *destroys both
the blameless and the wicked* (verse 22). This generalization
concisely refutes his friends' simplistic notion that God
always punishes the wicked and always blesses the weak.

Such despair leads Job to light a small candle of hope
in the midst of his darkness: Could there be an *arbitrator*
(verse 33) to control God in the courtroom? Job dismisses
the thought, but it will continually resurface (see 16:19;
19:25-27).

Rahab (verse 13) is another name for the sea monster,
Leviathan. Its *helpers* (NRSV; NIV *cohorts*) refer to other
powerful creatures under its control. Such beings
represented, mythologically, the chaos that had to be
controlled in order for Creation to occur. (See the
commentary on 3:8 and on chapter 41.)

Verse 18 is a repetition, in a different form, of 7:19.
God hounds Job relentlessly.

Verses 20-21: Bildad wanted Job to become *blameless* by
repenting of his sin. Job asserts that he is already
blameless, having committed no transgression.

Sudden death (verse 23) is the most shocking and

painful, occurring without preparation. God *mocks,* or laughs at, such tragedy.

Verse 24: Judges could control the wicked, but God maliciously renders them useless.

Verse 26 *speaks of* fragile, lightweight boats, capable of great speed.

Verse 27: Job refutes the "put on a happy face" method of dealing with pain.

In verses 32-35 Job allows himself to consider again the wish for a trial with God. *Umpire* (verse 33 NRSV; NIV, *someone to arbitrate*) carries the sense of a powerful judge who could take away God's *rod* (verse 34). Only Job's firm conviction of his innocence allows him to demand a confrontation with God in court.

Verse 35*b* means, "for I don't have confidence alone."

Job's Accusatory Prayer (10:1-22)

As in the closing of his preceding speech (7:7-21), Job ends this one with a prayer. Predictably, it is more biting than the last. He begins by demanding an answer to why God is persecuting him (verse 2). He next accuses the Lord of being totally unable to relate humanely to people (verses 3-7). To prove this, he uses himself as an example of God's irrational and brutal treatment (verses 8-19). He concludes the prayer with no request other than to be left alone (verses 20-22).

Verse 1 is almost a repetition of 7:11, which began the anger portion of his prayer. Whereas that prayer started with a humble introduction, however, this address to God begins with unrestrained rage.

Verse 2b: This question underscores Job's bewilderment. He cannot understand why God is turning from kind friend to vicious enemy.

To describe God's irrational treatment of him, Job uses two images. God is a potter, carefully making a vessel and then flippantly destroying it (verses 8-12). God is also a hunter, treating the defenseless Job as if he were a dangerous lion (verses 13-17).

Compare verse 9 to 7:7.

Verse 10 is a poetic description of conception and of the growth of a fetus in the womb.

These things (verse 13 NRSV; NIV, *this is what*) refers to what follows: Job's helplessness in the face of God's arrows.

Verse 16 uses a traditional phrase in Hebrew literature descriptive of God's acts on behalf of Israel (see 1 Chronicles 16:22, 24). Job's use of the phrase overflows with sarcasm: God's miracles are seen in the suffering inflicted upon him.

Witnesses (verse 17) may refer to Job's former companions who now scoff at him (see 19:13-19 and 30:1-14).

Verses 18-19: Job repeats his desire for an early death, given the current suffering (see 3:11-12, 16).

Verses 20-22: Job repeats his request from his earlier prayer (7:16*b*)—*Let me alone!* Observe the New Revised Standard Version footnote on the Hebrew term translated *comfort* (NIV: *a moment's joy*) It literally means *brighten up.* If God will stop sending senseless suffering, then Job may enjoy some "light" before going to Sheol, the abode of the dead (see the commentary on 7:9). That realm is the land of gloom and chaos, where light is like darkness.

§ § § § § § §

The Message of Job 8–10

Job is traveling down a road leading him farther and farther from his theological home. He grew up with an all-powerful, all-knowing God. We have seen in these chapters that the sufferer has reached the point of rejecting such a God. *Rejecting* is actually too mild a term: Job is *rebelling* violently. Behind the epithets hurled at God in chapters 9–10 is Job's feeling that this Almighty Being can turn maliciously capricious.

This raises the question for us, *What kind of a God do we look for to help us?* Our initial wish may be for a deity Job used to be at home with—the "immortal, invisible, God only wise" type. Perhaps we will find, like Job, that a God totally absolute is, in some respects, incapable of giving us what we need.

What kind of God do we need, then? It is the God Job will find at the end of his journey. He is beginning to see a faint form when he desires an *umpire* (9:33). He wants to be able to talk face-to-face with God. He wants to ask God questions and understand the answers. In other words, Job wants a God who is compassionately accessible.

When we endure a tragedy, only some of the pain is physical or emotional. The other part is spiritual. We ask our own "whys." "Why are you doing this to me, God?" "Why don't things make sense any more?" We do not hear any answers because our old God is gone and the new one is in the fetal stage. The fact that we cry, however, shows that we are in transition. Our suffering has caused us to leave home and embark upon a dangerous journey. We are afraid. But we are walking beside Job.

§ § § § § § §

Job 11–14

Introduction to These Chapters

The first speeches of the friends serve to introduce us to their personalities. While all three agree with the orthodox view of divine reward/punishment, they vary in how they try to persuade Job. Eliphaz boldly claims direct revelation, while Bildad appeals to tradition.

In this third friend's introductory speech, Zophar brandishes yet another weapon in the war to defeat Job's arrogance: knowledge. He refers to the *secrets of wisdom* (11:6), and mentions the *deep things of God* (11:7 NRSV; NIV *the mysteries of God*). He closes his short address with a very logical *if . . . then* sermon (11:13-20).

Knowing a lot about things and little about people, Zophar bluntly and perhaps blindly tramples on Job's feelings. He sees Job's outcries only as a base for theological debate, callously calling them a *multitude of words* (11:2 NRSV; NIV *all these words*) and *babble* (11:3 NRSV; NIV *idle talk*). He scolds Job by saying that the sufferer deserves more than what God has delivered (11:6c). He discounts the horror his friend is enduring when he blithely tells him, *You will forget* (11:16). Zophar is totally incapable of understanding the depth of human suffering.

Job's response serves as a watershed point in the book. Reflecting its importance, it encompasses three chapters (12-14)—the longest speech in the dialogue section.

In this discourse, Job makes a two-part move. He first

(chapters 12-13) breaks completely from his friends. It should be noted that in his response to Bildad (see Part 4 of the commentary), he did not lash out at his comforters. It was as if he still hoped they would turn from arguing to consoling. Given Zophar's stinging insensitivity, though, Job now realizes that they are as cold and immovable as granite.

The structure of chapters 12 and 13 reflects this sad realization. Both chapters share a framework that is unlike any other in terms of expressing pure anger and anguish:

- insult of friends (12:2-5; 13:1-2)
- assertion (12:6; 13:3)
- renewed insult of friends (12:7-12; 13:4-12)
- return to assertion (12:13-25; 13:13-27)

Job cannot contain his hurt. He is trying to get his ideas across, but his emotions get in the way. By his continual return to raging at his friends, he is severing all bonds with them.

Just as he turns away from the three men, in chapter 14 he turns toward God. He realizes that his only hope is with the Almighty, yet this deity is the cause of his suffering. Timidly—hesitantly—he alternates between talking to himself and addressing God:

- statement (verses 1-2)
- prayer (verses 3-6)
- statement (verses 7-12)
- prayer (verses 13-17)
- statement (verses 18-19*a*)
- accusation (verses 19*b*-20)
- statement (verses 21-22)

In his remaining speeches Job will continue speaking to his friends. But—with rare exception (19:21-22) he will speak only to dismiss them. His struggle will be with God.

In terms of critical considerations, 13:28 appears misplaced. It should be read in the context of the opening verses of chapter 14, possibly after verse 2.

Here is an outline of the content of chapters 11-14:

Condemnation of Job (11:1-6)

As in the opening of Bildad's speech (8:2), Zophar reveals how Job's words have affected him. The third friend is angry and feels compelled to answer.

Verse 3 is ironic, since the three friends will be *silenced* by the end of the book. (See 32:3, 5.)

Zophar refers, in verse 4, to Job's words in 9:15, 20-21. Note that this is his interpretation of what Job is saying. He reduces things to an intellectual debate by putting in Job's mouth the academic term, *doctrine.*

Verse 6: See the commentary on 4:21 for a discussion concerning *wisdom.*

God's Knowledge and Justice (11:7-12)

Consistent with his intellectual bent, Zophar stumbles ahead by refuting what he feels is wrong with Job's *doctrine.* Contradicting Job's views in chapter 9, he asserts that God's pure knowledge and unimpeachable justice are consistent with each other. He does not prove this, however: Believing any other way is unthinkable.

In the Hebrew view of the universe, *heaven* was the region above the earth. The *heavens* thus means the farthest point from the human world. This contrasts to *Sheol,* the area underneath the earth (see the commentary on 7:9).

Compare verse 10 with 9:11. Zophar uses Job's image, but praises God's power.

Verse 12 is an ancient proverb illustrating the impossibility of some people (Job?) gaining understanding.

"If . . . Then" Sermon (11:13-20)

Zophar sees the solution to Job's pain in simplistic terms. *If* Job repents (verses 13-14), *then* he will prosper once again (verses 15-19). The latter verses reflect Zophar's research into Job's condition; they are paraphrases of Job's earlier complaints, turned by the friend into statements of hope (verse 15—10:16; verse 16—3:24; verses 17—10:20-22; verse 18—7:6; verse 19—7:3-4).
Not surprisingly, the sermon concludes with a threat (verse 20).

Verses 13-14: The ancient Hebrews connected outward expression *(hand)* and inner disposition *(heart)*. What was in a person's hand was symbolic of what was in the heart (see Isaiah 1:15).

Lift up your face (verse 15) is an action of hope and faith (see Psalms 24:7; 121:1).

Verse 20c is a thinly veiled reference to Job. The sufferer has already voiced his desire for death (3:11-12; 10:18-19).

God's Whimsical Rule (12:1—25)

Job dismisses his friend's theology by affirming the obvious: God's rule in human affairs appears arbitrary. As noted in the introduction, this theologizing is laced with insults directed at the friends. See the structure of chapter 12 outlined there.

Wisdom will die with you (verse 2) has a meaning relevant to the political situation of Judah (see the Introduction, "How the Book Was Written"). In light of the national catastrophe, people continuing to think in traditional theological terms *will* doom wisdom.

I am not inferior to you (verse 3) strikes at the heart of

Job's anger at his friends. They are treating him as if he is ignorant of their beliefs, when in fact he knows them better than they. This theology is empty and useless to him now, yet the friends keep bombarding him with it. Such *things* refer to Job's pain as outlined in verse 4.

And he answered me (verse 4) may be taken sarcastically. When Job prayed for relief, God answered with more persecution.

Verse 5: Job accuses his friends of speaking from their context of *ease,* with no sensitivity to his situation of pain. He repeats this charge in 16:4.

In verse 6 Job asserts God's injustice, then immediately returns to condemning the friends. He will resume his assertion in verse 13. *Who bring their god in their hand* refers to idolators.

Verses 7-8: Plants and animals recognize the Almighty's misuse of power, but Zophar and his companions are blind to it.

Verse 12 is meant sarcastically. Considering the three men's inability to see what even dumb creatures understand, Job smirks: *Wisdom is with the aged?*

In verses 13-25 Job observes God's acts of toppling nations and those in power. Ordinarily one would expect affirmation of God's justice in those acts, but Job omits this. He is affirming the opposite, that there is no justice whatsoever. As in verse 2, this passage has its roots in the national catastrophe experienced by the poet. It may be the scene the poet witnessed as the Babylonians raped his homeland.

Verse 25 may be a reference to the Babylonian practice of blinding the leaders of conquered countries (see 2 Kings 25:7).

Plea for Confrontation with God (13:1-27)

Having dismissed any possibility of God's justice in dealing with humanity, Job boldly voices his desire to *see God in court.* Recall, though, that he is still raging at his friends, and this anger gets in the way of cool thinking (see the structure of the chapter outlined in the Introduction).

In the midst of this reflecting and raging, Job cannot help addressing God (verses 20-27). Even though the Almighty may be unjust, Job is more hopeful of understanding coming from God than from his friends.

Compare verses 1-2 with 12:3. Job is still fuming over the empty condescension of his friends.

Verse 3: This is his assertion, which he will resume in verse 13.

Verse 7-11: Job condemns his friends for showing *partiality* to God. Does God need such defending, where a person will ignore the obvious and ascribe to the Lord a questionable righteousness? The three men will eventually be required to atone for this; the prophecy in verse 10*a* will be fulfilled in 42:7-9.

Verse 12: Job counters Zophar's ancient proverb (11:12) with one of his own.

Verse 13: *Let me have silence.* Job's friends may be about to reply to his harsh comments.

My flesh in my teeth (verse 14 NRSV) is a phrase found only here, referring to Job putting his life on the line (cf. NIV) in what he is about to say. *My life in my hand* emphasizes the same thing (see Judges 12:3).

Verse 16: Only a righteous person may come before God. There is, thus, hope for Job—but it is slim.

His friends cannot contend with him (verses 19-21). Job maintains that God may do so, but only if two conditions are met: God must stop hurting him, and Job's paralyzing fear of the Almighty must be taken away.

Verses 23-27 describe things Job would ask of God, referring back to verse 22*b*. It is possible that he is beginning to acknowledge that there could be past sins for which he is now paying. He is still not aware of any. If such acknowledgment will get God to court, though, he is willing to open himself to the possibility! In these verses, Job's faint hope melts into anger.

Verse 24: Job, as in 10:2, again asks the central question: *Why* is God an enemy, no longer a friend?

Lament and Prayer (13:28-14:22)

In this chapter, where Job alternates between talking to himself and beseeching God, he allows himself to hope. The section concludes, though, with an emotion well known to him: despair.

Verses 13:28-14:2: As noted in the introduction, 13:28 may best be read after 14:2. Job's reflection upon the fleeting character of humanity drives him to address God in the following verses.

Verse 6: Job renews his plea (10:20) of wanting God to leave him alone. Note the change from his view in 7:1-2 regarding the *hired laborer:* Job would now gladly settle for a servant's life.

Verses 7-12: The sufferer briefly entertains the thought of a "generic" afterlife for all, a common Egyptian belief. He quickly dismisses it, however.

Verses 13-17: A new thought suddenly strikes Job. Perhaps after Job's death, and after God's *wrath* has subsided, God will *remember* him. The Lord may then, just for Job, restore the relationship they once enjoyed.

Regarding *Sheol* (verse 13 NRSV; NIV, *grave*), see the commentary on 7:9.

In verse 14*b* Job uses the hireling image of 14:6. *Release* may refer to when God, the master, turns from anger to compassion.

Compare verses 15-17 to 7:19-21, where Job feels there is no hope of receiving divine compassion.

Verses 18-19a: Job realizes there is no basis for his preceding "wishful thinking."

Verses 19b-22: How can Job believe that God will turn away from bullying him? God has proved to be a relentless tyrant who will take away the hope of any person, living or dead.

§ § § § § § §

The Message of Job 11–14

How does one talk to a sufferer? This is a relevant question, now that all three friends have had opportunities to address Job. Job's reply to the last comforter gives a sharp answer, forged from fire that grew hotter with each word he heard.

Do not defend God! The companions, insulted by Job's blasphemies, try to "justify" God's dealings with him. On a theological level, this is absurd: If God is all-powerful, why is human defense necessary? On a personal level, this is insulting: Job's feelings, and his value as a person, are degraded. If the men had kept alive their affection for Job, and had spoken from the compassion of their hearts instead of from the callousness of their brains, then the sufferer would not be alone in his pain.

But he is, and this raises for him—and for us—another question: *How does one approach a mysterious God?* Feeling forsaken by his friends, and feeling that God is hounding him, Job could have ended things after 13:12. Something within him refuses to yield, however.

That something is a distant hope that God is more loving and just than his friends. He refuses to believe that God is as he fears. With timidity and fright he dares to hope. Once he starts, the floodgates open. The faint wish for an *arbitrater*, entertained in 9:33, he now expands into a gigantic scene; it is as if he is saying to himself, "What if I can confront God in a courtroom, and talk face to face with the Lord?" Carried away, he continues hoping: "What if God remembers me after I die, restores things the way they were, and allows me to live again?"

Certainly in our pain our friends—with the best of intentions—may nonetheless make our lives even more miserable. Confronted with this, *dare to hope that God may break through and surprise you with the unexpected.* Look at your situation and allow yourself to fantasize. Disregarding reality, what words would you like to hear? What things would you like to have happen? Whom would you like to see?

This in no way is "pie in the sky" daydreaming. You will still spend most of your time anxious and depressed. But allowing yourself to hope, even briefly, is not just healthy. It communicates to the shadowy God your special, personal needs. And that hope may be the vehicle by which the Lord will come to you.

§ § § § § § §

Job 15–17

Introduction to These Chapters

These chapters inaugurate the second cycle of
discourses in Job see "The Structure and Text of Job" in
the Introduction.

This second set of conversations between Job and the
three comforters contrasts starkly with the first. The
difference may be summed up in one sentence: The two
sides have given up on each other. Throughout the earlier
chapters, each speaker wanted the other to change. The
friends tried to persuade Job to confess his sins and
repent. Job wanted his companions to stop giving him
theology lectures and start showing compassion.

In the series of speeches beginning with chapter 15,
there is a realization that neither side will budge. It
would be more accurate to call these speeches
"monologues" rather than conversations. The men are
not concerned so much with listening to as with talking
past each other.

Eliphaz's second speech is a good example of this
practice of talking past each other. Gone are the courtesies
opening his first words to Job (4:1–5:27). Gone are the
"gentle nudgings" and the hopeful conclusion. In their
place are a brutal attack on Job's character and a
ponderous discourse on the fate of the wicked. There is
no doubt in his mind that Job is now beyond help. He is a
sinner who will never repent. Thus, the friend, who had
been characterized as the most compassionate, turns to

prattling callously the dogma of divine reward/ punishment.

As noted in Part 5, Job has already realized that his friends will be useful only as tormentors. His reply in chapters 16 and 17 reflects this revelation. Much as he did in his last address (chapters 12–14), he alternates between attacking them, on the one hand, and reflecting/praying, on the other. This switching back and forth makes his reply to Eliphaz somewhat difficult to follow, since it is unclear to whom Job is speaking: to his friends, to himself, or to God.

This difficult structure reflects the rage he still directs at his friends, who he feels have betrayed him. It also reflects the chaos in Job's heart. He is buffeted by swirling emotions, making a neat, systematic speech impossible. Job is a despairing, confused man, and his sometimes befuddled words in chapters 16 and 17 demonstrate this.

The sufferer, though, has not totally given up. Throughout his earlier speeches he had expressed a vague hope. He wished for an *arbitrater* (9:33) who would hold God in check. He also longed for a court date with God (13:3, 18-27). Similarly, in his speech here, he expresses the hope of having a *witness in heaven* who can testify to God regarding his character (16:19). Job's hope still rests in his belief in his innocence and in his confidence that God is acting unjustly.

In turning to critical considerations of these chapters, two verses seem out of place: 16:20 and 17:12. Both verses criticize the friends, and both abruptly appear in the middle of passages dealing with other matters. While some scholars judge them to have originally occurred elsewhere (possibly after 17:2), it is important to note, as seen above, that throughout this speech Job alternates his audience. Thus such verses could be seen as "asides," where he purposely interrupts his train of thought, looks at his friends, and lashes out at them.

Here is an outline of chapters 15–17.

I. Eliphaz's Second Speech (15:1-35)
  A. Insult of Job (15:1-6)
  B. Condemnation of Job's arrogance (15:7-16)
  C. The fate of the wicked (15:17-35)
II. Job's Reply (16:1-17:16)
  A. Outrage at his friends (16:1-6)
  B. Outrage at God (16:7-14)
  C. Despairing cry for hope (16:15-17:5)
  D. Concluding lament (17:6-16)

Insult of Job (15:1-6)

It is helpful to compare these verses to 4:2-6, Eliphaz's opening words to Job. The tenor of this friend's speech has now taken a 180-degree turn, setting the stage for the types of discourses we may expect in this second cycle of speeches. Eliphaz directly accuses Job of sinning (see verse 5); consequently, the friend does not hesitate to condemn him.

In his use of the word *wise* (verse 2), Eliphaz is referring to 12:3 and 13:2, where Job is claiming wisdom. He is using the phrase sarcastically, since a true wise man would never *answer with windy knowledge* (NRSV; NIV, *empty notions;* see also 8:2). *East wind* refers to a sirocco, a hot desert wind that destroys vegetation. Job's reasoning, thus, is destructive, like a sirocco, and must be curtailed.

Fear of God (verse 4 NRSV; NIV, *devotion to God*), descriptive of one's proper attitude to the Almighty, is an especially important theme for Eliphaz. He mentioned it twice, for example, in his first speech (4:6, 14). Eliphaz's anger stems from Job arrogantly defying God, thus kicking this sacred belief.

Verse 5: This is the oriental way of describing how one's actions are tied to one's character (see also 11:13).

Verse 6: As if self-conscious about the harshness with

which he has just spoken, Eliphaz feels the need to
explain: Job has brought it on himself.

Condemnation of Job's Arrogance (15:7-16)

Eliphaz repeats the essence of his theme in 4:12-21,
where he contrasted God's power to humanity's weakness.
In keeping with brutalizing Job, though, Eliphaz here
personalizes things: Job is small in comparison to God, so
what right does he have to be so rebellious?

Verse 7 may refer to the Creation story, where the *first
man* consulted with God (Genesis 2:18–3:24).

Verse 8: Have you listened in the council of God? This is a
sarcastic way of asking Job if he has had a personal
conversation with the Almighty.

In verse 9 Eliphaz is mocking Job's hurt expressed in
12:3 and 13:2.

In verse 10 Eliphaz refers to himself, since he is the
eldest friend. Job's sarcasm in 12:12 angers him.

Verse 11 refers to the "gentleness" of his first speech.

The *heart* (verse 12) was viewed as the center of the
intellect. "Conscience" is a synonym.

Compare verses 14-16 with 4:18-20.

The Fate of the Wicked (15:17-35)

This section, like many found in the remaining
speeches of the friends, repeats—tediously—the
orthodox view of divine punishment of sinners. The
prevalent image is that of *darkness* (verses 22, 23, 30),
descriptive of the hopelessness of the wicked. Perhaps
Eliphaz picks this up from Job's first speech (3:4-6).

Verse 19 is not necessarily a reference to the conquest
of Canaan. Because of Eliphaz's non-Hebrew
background, he could be referring to an event in the
history of Tema, his homeland.

Eliphaz defines wickedness in terms of defiance to *the
Almighty* (verses 25-26)—precisely Job's "sin." Later he
will define it in social terms (22:5-9).

Fat (verse 27) was a sign of prosperity in ancient times.

Verse 28 is best understood as referring to the consequence of the wicked person in verses 25-27. It may be read as a new sentence and translated, "This wicked person will dwell in desolate cities."

Compare verse 35 to Psalm 7:14.

Outrage at His Friends (16:1-6)

Job had previously complained at length of his friends' insensitive theologizing (13:7-12). He now recalls, with words dripping with heavy sarcasm, a minor theme he alluded to earlier (12:5). His friends can readily preach because they are comfortable; if they were in Job's sandals, their views would be different.

Job begins as he did in 12:3 (repeated in 13:1-2)—he knows what his friends know. *Miserable comforters* (verse 2) is a satirical reference to the mission of his friends, as seen in 2:11.

Verse 5 is sarcastic, since his friends neither *encourage* him nor assuage his pain.

Outrage at God (16:7-14)

Having blasted his companions, he now turns his wrath toward God. In the same "no holds barred" attitude, he freely voices his feelings. In place of the love he once felt, he now states matter-of-factly that God hates him (verse 9). The reason for this decision is that his experience of God is similar to the experience of a city besieged by a ruthless band of warriors (verse 14).

Verse 8 is a description of Job's weakened physical condition.

The verb translated *hated* (verse 9 NRSV; NIV, *fears*) has similarities with the noun translated *the Satan* in the prose narrative (see the commentary on 1:6). Perhaps in Job's eyes, God and *the Satan* are indistinguishable! *Sharpens his eyes* (NRSV) suggests that God is scrutinizing Job in order to see where next to assault him (see NIV).

Verses 10-11: Job's social isolation is as painful as his physical suffering. It, too, is a sign of God's hatred.

Compare verse 12 to 7:20. Job sees himself as the focus of God's violent hatred.

He bursts upon me (verse 14) is a phrase signifying the breaks in the protective walls of a city, allowing invaders to enter.

Despairing Cry for Hope (16:15–17:15)

These difficult verses convey Job's attitude in light of the realization of his abandonment by both God and his friends. In the midst of his sadness, a hope for a *witness* (verse 19) defiantly rises within him.

The term *sackcloth* (verse 15) appears only here. It is a symbol not only of sorrow but also of humility and righteousness (see Psalm 35:13-14). *In the dust* refers to collapsing in total weakness, like a mighty animal that has been mortally wounded.

Verse 17 is an aside, as if directed at his friends. He wants them to know that he still maintains his innocence!

Verse 18: The spilled blood of an innocent person cries out for justice (see Genesis 4:10; 37:26). Thus, Job's blood is a symbol of God's injustice, and its *cry* should not be silenced until he is vindicated.

The *witness* (verse 19) is a divine being who, upon hearing the cry of the blood-stained earth, testifies to God of Job's innocence. Job does not have anyone in mind; this is only a wish.

Verse 20: See the introduction regarding this verse. It is best seen as an aside to his friends.

Verse 21 should be connected directly to verse 19. *He* refers to the divine witness, not to God.

Verses 16:22–17:1 underline the desperateness of Job's plight. He is about to die, and after his death a witness will be useless. Note the three short phrases in 17:1—this meter differs from the other verses and denotes the intensity of his despair, almost as if he is giving up and dying as he speaks.

Verses 2-5: In light of his *mockers* (his friends), Job asks God for a *pledge,* a promise wherein Job might be spared from further torment until his court date. This would at least silence them temporarily. However, he lapses into pessimism—no one can guarantee this (verse 3*b*). Perhaps the most Job can hope for is that God will not let his companions get away with their arrogance (verse 4).

Verse 5 is hopelessly corrupt. It is possibly proverbial, used by Job to criticize his friends' injustice.

Concluding Lament (17:6-16)

Job's hope for a divine witness and a silencing of his friends is ultimately ungrounded. It gives way, in light of the reality of his lonely suffering, to a lament.

Byword (verse 6) means that his name is used as a source of ridicule (see Psalms 44:14; 69:11). This is similar to his description of himself as a *laughingstock* in 12:4c.

The *eye* (verse 7) in Hebrew thought symbolized a person's orientation in the world (Isaiah 43:8). Job is affirming, thus, his confused state and weakening intellectual ability. The chaotic, rambling structure of his speech further indicates this.

In verses 8-9, the *upright, innocent,* and *righteous* may be sarcastic descriptions of the companions. Job is saying that they see themselves in such a pious light. Yet, if they were so holy, they would certainly be *wise* (verse 10; NIV; NRSV, *sensible*), which they are not.

Compare the structure of verse 11 to 17:1. Once again, the meter of the verse is descriptive of the staggered, staccato breath of a dying person.

See the critical comments in the Introduction regarding verse 12.

See the commentary on 7:9 regarding *Sheol* (verse 13 NRSV; NIV, *grave*).

Pit (verse 14 NRSV; NIV, *corruption*) is a descriptive term for the grave, used in many of the psalms (30:9; 94:13, for example). Job personifies the grave, as he does the *worm.*

We in verse 16 refers to Job and his hope.

§ § § § § § §

The Message of Job 15–17

These chapters give insight as to the effects of pain in our lives.

Suffering causes us to be angry. Although this may sound simplistic, it is important. Job unbridles his rage. Directed at both God and his friends, it provides a source of emotional energy. It drives him until he can posit hope in a divine witness.

Often we repress our natural feelings of anger. Perhaps by tapping those feelings we may find, like Job, strength to endure until we can hope again.

Suffering causes us to explore the nature of faith. The faith of Eliphaz and his companions insulates them from the reality of the world—as represented by the wretched Job. They have irrelevant answers for all relevant questions. Job's faith, on the other hand, challenges him to discard worn out views. Faith for him is a quest for a new vision of the Almighty.

We are faced with a decision. Will our faith insulate us from pain? Or will it challenge us to seek new answers that incorporate even senseless suffering?

Suffering causes us to see things more realistically. Eliphaz has no difficulty labeling the wicked. He also does not hesitate claiming that God always punishes them. He makes such declarations from a pain-free context. Job sees just the opposite. Having been cast as a sinner in the eyes of his friends, he knows that such labels can be deceptive. He also sees quite clearly that some of the most wicked of all people escape God's wrath.

Comfort makes us view things in a skewed way. When we run up against the hard, painful wall of suffering, though, reality confronts us.

§ § § § § § §

Job 18–19

Introduction to These Chapters

Bildad's first speech (chapter 8) to Job was biting. A fiery preacher by nature, this friend tried to persuade the sufferer through a "hellfire-and-brimstone" sermon.

As noted in Part 5, the second cycle of speeches is characterized by each side realizing that the other will not change. They consequently give up on each other. In Bildad's second speech (chapter 18), he retires his preaching role: Job will never repent.

Bildad, freed from needing to help Job see the light, now expresses himself freely. What he attempts is simple: Put Job in his proper place. He criticizes the sufferer for questioning the wisdom of him and the other two (18:2-4). He then fills the rest of his speech with several images descriptive of the fate of the wicked. These images, though, are but slightly veiled references to Job. His anger burns deeply, and one can almost detect glee in his voice as he paints the picture of destruction.

Bildad portrays himself as a pedantic and bitter man. There is little new in the address. On the contrary, in addition to harping again on the theme of divine punishment, he uses phrases similar to those in his first speech. He also cuts the speech short, as he did his first one. His anger, or the fact that he runs out of images, contributes to this.

Job's response (chapter 19) is both predictable and surprising. He responds to Bildad's insults with insults of his own (verses 2-3 and 28-29). He also continues indexing how God is pursuing him, a theme in his previous speech (16:11-14).

What is new in this discourse is that in the middle of it he collapses. His anger at his friends and at God had been enough to drive him in his defiance. But now we hear, *Have pity on me, have pity on me, O you my friends* (19:21*a*).

As he recalls how all have forsaken him, it is simply too much. His pride breaks, and he beseeches the three men—the ones who are his fiercest tormentors. He still needs human company.

It is important to note that as he tries to persuade them, he once again voices a heavenly hope. He expresses confidence in an emerging *Redeemer*, or vindicator (19:25). Earlier, he had hoped for an *arbitrater* (9:33) who could restrain God's power. He next dreamed of a *witness* who could vouch for him (16:19). Now, he looks toward a *Redeemer* who can administer justice (see the commentary on 19:25 below).

In terms of critical consideration, Bildad's speech is fairly clear, while Job's contains murky passages: Verses 4, 17, 20, and 26-27 are very difficult to understand. Their structure, along with their phrases, is so complicated that an accurate interpretation is impossible. They reflect the mind of a depressed and anxious man.

Here is an outline of chapters 18–19.
  I. Bildad's Second Speech (18:1-21)
      A. Rebuke of Job (18:1-4)
      B. The fate of the wicked (18:5-21)
  II. Job's Reply (19:1-29)
      A. Rebuke of friends (19:1-6)
      B. Lament of God's injustice (19:7-20)
      C. Expression of hope (19:21-29)

Rebuke of Job (18:1-4)

This rebuke reveals one of the reasons for Bildad's

anger. He feels Job is insulting him by not agreeing with his orthodox theology.

Verse 2 contains the opening phrase of his first speech (8:2). It should be noted that *you* is in the plural in Hebrew; it is possible that Bildad is addressing his two companions, wondering why they cannot silence the arrogant Job. If Bildad is addressing Job, the verse may refer to the difficulty with which Job is speaking, as evidenced by his disjointed speech in 16:1–17:16.

Cattle (verse 3) is perhaps a reference to Job's insult in 12:7 (see also Psalm 73:22).

Verse 4: *Tear yourself in anger.* Job is hurting himself, because of his sin; God is not the one tearing him apart. *Shall the earth be forsaken for you . . . ?* (NRSV; NIV, *is the earth to be abandoned . . .*). This is another way of saying, "Should God change everything just for you?"

The Fate of the Wicked (18:5-21)

Bildad throws together varied descriptions of the wicked person's experiences. These include darkness (verses 5-6, 18), entrapment (verses 7-10), *terrors* (verses 11, 14), disease (verses 12-13), and no legacy (verses 16-17, 19). The predominant image holding these together is that of the *tent* (verses 6, 14-15, 21): The state of a person's dwelling signifies the state of the person's life.

There is no order to this description. It is as if Bildad simply wants to paint a picture, and let Job draw his own conclusions. The model for this painting is, of course, Job himself.

Fire (verses 5-6) is a person's only protection from the terrors lurking in the night.

Bildad hints at a "natural" punishment of the sinner: His own schemes throw him down (verses 7-10). He does not pursue this, however. He focuses instead on comparing the fate of the wicked person to the fate of an animal subdued by the wares of a hunter: *net, trap, snare, rope* (NRSV; NIV, *noose*),

A healthy person takes long *steps* (verse 7*a*).

The term translated *terrors* (verses 11-13) is more general than the one in 6:14. It is used here and elsewhere (24:17; 27:20; 30:15) to refer to life-threatening powers suddenly falling upon a person. Specifically, such terrors include hunger, calamity, and disease. The *first-born of death* is a poetic description of disease.

King of terrors, mentioned in verse 14, may refer to a pagan god of the underworld thought to be responsible for death.

Sulfur (verse 15) is symbolic of divine retribution (see Genesis 19:24).

Verses 16-19 indicate the totality of death for the wicked. Not only will the sinner die, but the sinner's memory among the living will also die.

Verse 18 is an allusion to the dead descending into Sheol, the underworld (see 10:20-22).

East and *west* (verse 20), taken together, refer to the entire world.

The harshest insult of all to Job is that he does not know God (verse 21*b*).

Rebuke of Friends (19:1-6)

Although these verses criticize his friends, the anger has receded. The predominant tone, in keeping with the rest of the chapter, is one of lament: Job is saying, in essence, "Look at what is happening to me, and how you've hurt me!"

Job begins by sarcastically using Bildad's expression, *how long* (see 18:2). Compare *break me in pieces* (NRSV; NIV, *crush me*) with 18:4.

Ten times (verse 3) is a poetic way of saying *repeatedly* (see Numbers 14:22). The phrase is not to be taken literally.

Discovering the exact meaning of verse 4 is impossible. It may mean that only Job knows whether or not he has sinned; his friends, who are accusing him, have no such knowledge. It may also mean, taken in light of the following verses, that God is making Job's "sin" remain with him; hence, there are unjust grounds for continued persecution.

Job's friends may be blaming Job, but they should blame God, since God is unjustly dealing with him (verses 5-6). *Net* may refer to the ancient pagan creation legend. The sea monster Leviathan, symbolic of chaos, was trapped in the net of a god (see the commentary on 3:8 and on chapter 41).

Lament of God's Injustice (19:7-20)

Job further elaborates on this theme from his previous speech (16:7-14). He continues viewing God as a vicious soldier relentlessly attacking him (verses 7-12). The intensity with which Job feels this violence is conveyed in the brutal language he uses. God has walled up, set darkness, stripped, taken, uprooted, and kindled.

In verses 13-20 Job lingers on the last and most painful horror thrown at him by the rampaging deity: the curse of a life devoid of any family or social support. Note the totality of the loneliness experienced by Job in this section. He mentions all those who could possibly lend support but do not.

Verse 7: Job no longer believes the one thing he previously thought undeniable, namely, that the Almighty is a deity of *justice.* God has forsaken the cause of the powerless.

Compare *walled up my way* (verse 8) to *hedged in,* 3:23.

Verse 9: See Psalm 8:5 and Proverbs 14:24.

Compare *he breaks me down* (verse 10) to *he breaks me with breach upon breach* (16:14). *My hope* may refer to his children (see 18:16-19).

Verse 12: The soldier imagery of God, a favorite of Job, runs throughout the book. (See 10:17; 16:14; 30:12.)

The difficulty with verse 17 is seen in comparing the NRSV and NIV translations with the KJV: *My breath is strange to my wife, though I entreated for the children's sake of my own body.* Many scholars feel the rendering in the KJV is more accurate. Job is describing the repulsiveness of his appearance: the stench of his horrible breath and decaying body. This description parallels verse 20, where Job returns to describing his body. Such descriptions point to God's wrath.

The first part of verse 20 has roots in some lament psalms (see Psalm 22:17). It is a graphic depiction, along with other places in Job (2:7; 7:5; 16:8; 30:17, 30), describing the results of the disease ravaging him. The phrase in the second part of the verse has become a modern proverb. It may mean that he is starving to death because his teeth have fallen out and he can only eat with the *skin* of his teeth, namely, his gums.

Expression of Hope (19:21-29)

Job has frightened himself with the preceding description of his lonely plight. It is more than he can bear. Desperately overlooking his knowledge that his friends will never change, he grovels before them, pleading for understanding companionship (verses 21-22). In an almost bizarre turn, he tries to force them to help him. He asserts in the remaining verses (23-29) that he will be justified after all. His friends, hence, should show compassion or they will meet the *sword* of divine wrath (verse 29). This foreshadows the conclusion of the book (42:7-10).

This request must have stunned his friends, since Job is irrationally asking them to abandon their theology. They believe that no one should befriend one who has been touched by the *hand of God* (verse 21).

Verse 22b carries the meaning, "Why do you verbally abuse me, seeing that I am suffering enough in the flesh?"

In verses 23-24 Job is forcefully expressing his certainty in his own innocence.

Although *Redeemer (Vindicator)* sometimes refers to

God (see Isaiah 63:16), it also refers to a relative who avenges a person who has been wronged (2 Samuel 14:11) and to one who administers justice on behalf of the weak (Proverbs 23:10-11). It should here (verse 25) be seen in the context of Job's earlier desire for a divine being who can stand up to God on his behalf.

Verses 26-27. These notoriously difficult verses seem to express the hope that God—after being confronted by the Redeemer—will turn favorably to Job. The sufferer again voices his irrational desire for a life after death; compare this to 14:13-17. Perhaps because he senses the impossibility of this, he expresses his impatience for the work of his Redeemer: *My heart faints* (NRSV; NIV, *yearns*) *within me!*

His friends' "sin" is not just found in their hurting him. It also lies in their belief that Job is guilty: *The root of the matter is found in him* (verse 28b; NRSV; NIV, *the root of the trouble is found in him*).

§ § § § § § §

The Message of Job 18–19

In contrast to the companions, Job is dynamic. Bildad spews out his anger, uses hackneyed phrases, and sits down. Job, on the other hand, explores his feelings and his faith. He talks not in traditional phrases but in new expressions. He can flash fire, or he can cry for mercy. His hurt has pushed him into an openness that makes him more fully human than his friends. Job, near death, is more alive than his comfortable companions.

We are the most spiritual when we feel we have nothing to lose. Seeking security so much that we confront present suffering with old beliefs turns us into stiff, cardboard, Bildad-like people. It is liberating knowing that only something new will save us. We filter things through new feelings, radical thoughts, emerging beliefs. Like Job we appear jumbled, confused, and inconsistent. But only then can we appreciate and appropriate God's grace.

There is a constant in our search for help: *We cannot escape our need for human companionship.* It should not be surprising to see Job beseeching men who respond to him with the compassion of a wall. Loneliness multiplies suffering. Silence makes us focus upon ourselves. Perhaps tormentors like Job's companions—and like friends who do not understand our situations—provide inadvertent help simply by drawing us out of private musings. Even uncompassionate companionship is better than none.

Similarly, *more important than even companionship is maintaining integrity.* In any crisis, there are things we call our own: feelings, beliefs, thoughts, actions. Open to our own reflection, they are still part of us. To diminish or abandon any of them cuts us off from the one thing that anchors us, namely, our sense of who we are.

§ § § § § § §

Job 20–21

Introduction to These Chapters

Zophar painted an academic portrait of himself in his first speech (chapter 11). It was a caricature of a highly intellectual man with little ability to understand or deal with human emotions. His second speech (chapter 20) deepens this picture's lines and colors.

Job has just made a final, impassioned appeal to his friends. Dropping his pride, he asked them for mercy (19:21). For Zophar to respond in the manner Job wants, he needs to know the language of compassion. He answers, instead, in a dialect well known to him: *My thoughts urge me* (NRSV; NIV, *prompt me*) *to answer me . . .* (20:2a); *a spirit beyond my understanding answers me* (20:3b NRSV; NIV, *my understanding inspires me to reply*).

His words come from the mind, a mind severed from the heart.

Zophar has not heard Job's appeal. He has, rather, been thinking of Job's earlier speech (chapters 16-17), where the sufferer has accused God of injustice. His speech, thus, is an intellectual response concerned—once again—with defending God's honor.

In a move worthy of his academic skill, he subtly tags a new twist onto the doctrine of divine punishment. Instead of merely proclaiming the horrible fate of the wicked, he suggests that such sinners may actually enjoy a somewhat nice life. It may thus appear that they go unpunished, as Job noted in 12:14-24. However, they will encounter God's justice, and their fate will be a nightmare: *Though his pride reaches to the heavens, and his head reaches to the clouds, he will perish for ever like his own dung* (20:6-7*a* NIV).

Although throughout his speech there are veiled references to Job, Zophar does not lash out at his hurting friend. Gone is the "introductory insult" characteristic of earlier speeches. Zophar is giving a cool, restrained, dispassionate response.

Job's answer (chapter 21), at first, also appears restrained. This is deceiving. His speech drips with sarcasm, barely covering his deep hurt at his friends' callousness. For example, there is no overt insult of his friends at the beginning of the speech. He says, *Listen carefully to my words, and let this be your consolation* (21:2).

The message is clear: "You can console me best by simply being quiet and listening!"

Job spends most of his speech directly contradicting Zophar's defense of God's justice. He has little difficulty citing examples where there is no punishment befitting a wicked person's deeds. The phrases he uses, though, are taken from verses in Psalms and Proverbs that depict the punishment of the wicked: 21:13 (Psalm 31:17); 21:14 (Psalm 25:2); 21:15 (Psalm 2:11-12); 21:17*a* (Proverbs 24:20); 21:17*b* (Proverbs 24:16); 21:18 (Psalm 1:4). Twisting these phrases of his friends, phrases rooted in Wisdom Literature, shows the utter disgust Job has for those who try to justify God at all costs.

Critically speaking, other than the characteristic obscure terms found occasionally, these chapters do not present major problems. Some verses appear out of context (see 21:16*b*; 21:22), but these do not affect the meaning of the ideas being expressed.

Here is an outline of chapters 20–21.

  I. Zophar's Second Speech (20:1-29)
    A. Introductory remarks (20:1-3)
    B. Brief prosperity of the wicked (20:4-29)

II. Job's Reply (21:1-34)
   A. Introductory remarks (21:1-6)
   B. Long-term prosperity of the wicked (21:7-34)

Zophar's Introductory Remarks (20:1-3)

Zophar appears agitated as he begins his speech. Some have interpreted these opening verses as meaning that Job has caused him to doubt his beliefs. It is more likely, though, that his agitation rises from the sufferer's blasphemy, and he is anxious to respond.

Verse 3 is Zophar's poetic way of expressing his urgency to reply to Job; compare it with verse 2a. Zophar is not thinking in terms of being divinely inspired, as did Eliphaz (4:12-17).

Brief Prosperity of the Wicked (20:4-29)

There are two main sections in this passage. The first, verses 4-22, contains his new thought, namely, that the wicked will not enjoy prosperity very long. The reason for such punishment is found in verses 19-22: The wicked person *has crushed and abandoned the poor* (NRSV; NIV, *oppressed* and *left destitute*). The remainder of the chapter (verses 23-29) is filled with images depicting the horrors God will visit upon such a sinner.

Verses 6-10: The evil person, trying to build a lasting name, will discover just the opposite. The remembrance of the sinner will be obliterated.

Compare *vision of the night* in verse 8 to 4:13.

Instead of dying old and *full of days* (42:17 NRSV; NIV, *years*), the evil person will die while still young (verse 11).

Verses 12-18: Just as the evil person tries to make a name (see above), the sinner accumulates a surplus of possessions. *Food* is at the pinnacle of the material mountain. The final food he or she will taste, however, is God's wrath.

One of the joys of such a person is plotting and

scheming to get more. A fitting punishment will be doing all this and not enjoying any reward, or *profit* (verse 18).

Verse 19: Job's companions had previously defined wickedness in terms of bidding defiance *to the Almighty* (15:25), which fits Job perfectly. Defining sin in terms of social and economic oppression has been only slightly touched upon before (see 5:15-16). This idea will be elaborated upon—to the point of absurdity—in Eliphaz's next speech (22:5-9).

Verses 22-28 show how thoroughly he has done his homework. The images Zophar chooses correspond to Job's earlier words: verses 24-25 (16:12-14); verse 26 (17:7); verse 27 (16:19). Zophar's point is to make sure Job sees himself unmistakably in the *tent* of the wicked.

A fire not *fanned* (verse 26b) probably refers to lightning.

Arrogantly, Zophar concludes his speech by stating that he has clearly described God's ways of dealing with sinners. By implication, Job can have no help whatsoever from the Almighty.

Job's Introductory Remarks (21:1-6)

As stated in the Introduction, these verses do not brim with violence—especially compared to the opening remarks in his earlier speeches (16:1-6; 19:1-6). It is as if Job is consciously imitating the professor-like style of Zophar. This makes the sarcasm found in these verses even more biting.

The main point behind these remarks is to express his bitterness at the realization, again, that his friends are useless as comforters.

See the Introduction regarding verse 2. The best the friends can do for Job is to keep silent.

Verse 3: Job sees things realistically. When his friends talk again, they will only *mock on.* The sufferer is not hearing his companions' speeches as benign lectures. Because they are speaking from their comfortable situations (16:4), their words are insulting to him.

Job's *complaint* (verse 4) is against God. He cannot get immediate satisfaction, so he is *impatient*. A complaint against a *human* may be resolved more readily.

As in 13:13-14, verses 5-6 let the listeners know that what Job is about to say will be shocking. Verse 6*a* refers to the blasphemy he preaches in the remainder of the chapter.

Long-term Prosperity of the Wicked (21:7-34)

The forthcoming shocking statement implied in verses 5-6 is made bluntly in verse 7: *Why do the wicked live on*, reach old age, and grow mighty *in power*? The blasphemous assumption behind this is that God acts unjustly.

Job fills the remainder of the chapter by contradicting Zophar's assertions regarding the short-lived prosperity of the wicked. He painstakingly catalogues his friend's statements and directly responds to them:

Zophar's Statements	Job's Replies
20:10-11	21:7-8
20:15	21:9
20:21	21:13
20:23, 28	21:17*b*
20:26a	21:17a

Like Zophar, Job has done his homework. His belief that God acts unjustly is based on careful, and sad, observations of the world around him.

Verse 16b: This affirmation of the righteous (compare with 22:18) seems strange coming from Job. It may have been an interjection by a later writer who was shocked by Job's denunciation of God's justice and retribution. Such an editor felt the need for a pious statement. It should be noted, however, that the phrase, *counsel of the wicked* (NIV; NRSV, *plans of . . .*), is also found in Psalm 1:1. Job may be talking sarcastically, in keeping with his other "impious" references to psalms and proverbs (see the Introduction).

In verse 19*a* Job cites the ancient view of children

being punished for the sins of their parents (see Exodus 34:7; Deuteronomy 5:9; Psalm 109:9-15).

Verses 19b-21: If God is just, why doesn't God punish the sinner instead of the sinner's children? As Job accurately notes, *What do they care for their houses after they die?* (verses 19b-21). If the wicked person has lived long and prosperously, how does persecuting the children punish the dead sinner?

Similar to verse 16b, some see verse 22 as a comment inserted later by a pious writer. However, this verse has similarities to Psalm 94:2, 10. Job may be speaking sarcastically.

Verse 24: These are images of prosperity (see 15:27; Proverbs 3:8).

Verses 27-28: Job sees through Zophar's veiled references to him. *Prince* (NRSV; NIV, *great man*) is the friend's sarcastic reference to Job. He is deprived of a *house* or *tent;* such deprivation is a sign of God's judgment against the *wicked,* according to Zophar (20:26, 28).

Those who travel (verses 29-30) refers to ordinary people: "Just ask anyone you meet. . . . " Job's thought is similar to that in 12:7-11, where he instructs his friends to learn what the creatures of nature already know. In other words, Job is telling his friends to use common sense when they look around them: The wicked are *spared in the day of calamity.*

Keeping watch over a grave (verse 32) signified that the deceased was rich and powerful.

Verse 33: Burials often took place in *valleys* (see Deuteronomy 34:6). The wicked person who receives such a peaceful and honorable death is not the exception. Countless others have lived and died the same way!

Zophar defended God in his previous speech. Job declares that defense to have been based on nothing but a *falsehood* (verse 34). Consequently, the only thing the friends offer Job is *nonsense* (NIV; NRSV, *empty nothings*).

§ § § § § § §

The Message of Job 20–21

It is impossible not to be impressed by the sustained coldness of Job's companions. Zophar must work at ignoring the sufferer's earlier pleas for compassion. To respond to those pleas with a cold theological discourse betrays a basic fact about how a comfortable friend may relate to a suffering one.

At the deepest level, a comforter prefers to stay on safe ground when relating to a sufferer. Zophar grasps at straws when he suggests the "delayed" punishment of the wicked. It makes little sense, as Job points out. It keeps him, though, from being swept into his friend's quagmire. Likewise, a person relating to you in your pain will, eventually, say absurd things. He or she will believe them. Those beliefs help preserve the person's sanity.

The statements made by the comforter may appear as "mockings" to the sufferer. Zophar's comments, at best, are just insensitive. They are not directly insulting to Job. Yet, the sufferer hears them as ridicule (21:3). Job knows the real issue: "Will you leave your comfortable world and sit with me awhile?" Zophar's intellectualism is absurd to Job. It says that Zophar does not take Job's situation seriously. Even if he did, he would not—could not—forsake his beliefs to join the sufferer. The whole scene is repugnant.

When you encounter pain, you have enough to worry about. Friends should realize that their attempts to cheer you up, to help you see the light, will not be heard rationally by you. The comments will be filtered through ears that want to hear the footsteps of one daring to venture defenselessly onto your turf.

The beginning of compassion is when the comforter believes he or she can learn from the sufferer. Job sees things around him clearly. His simple insights concerning the escape of the wicked from divine punishment are part of the vision that will eventually lead to a closer, more honest relationship with the Almighty. If Zophar had listened to them, he, too, might have gained a stronger and more realistic faith.

The one approaching you in your pain should not be frightened. Rather, he or she should be willing to listen to your story, your view. By listening instead of lecturing, you may both discover the new face of God.

§ § § § § § §

Job 22–24

Introduction to These Chapters

Each of the first two series of speeches had its own
motif (see the introduction to Part 6). It is impossible,
however, to generalize about the speeches found in the
third group (chapters 22–27). As will be seen in Part 10,
the conversations in this cycle are fragmented, presenting
many difficulties.

Eliphaz's third speech and Job's reply, chapters 22–24,
are the most nearly complete that will be found. If the
rest of the conversations in the third cycle were similar to
this interchange, a tendency would surface. In trying to
prove their belief in divine reward of the righteous and
punishment of the wicked, the friends grow increasingly
absurd and contradictory. Job, meanwhile, continues
expressing his thoughts and feelings straightforwardly.

Eliphaz sermonizes in chapter 22, a style he used in his
first address (chapters 4–5). Whereas in that earlier
homily he was poised and self-confident, though, this
last speech reveals no such composure. His rapidly
unraveling argument reflects this.

He begins by baldly asserting God's independence
from persons—no one can claim anything from the
Almighty (verses 2-4). He asserts this so strongly that his
later exhortation to Job to agree with God and accept
instruction (verses 21-22) makes little sense. How can a
good person honestly expect anything from a God who is

so untouchable? Eliphaz's defense of God's mysterious ways blows up in his face.

Perhaps the most dramatic—and absurd—example of the friend's failing logic is his description of Job's sins (verses 6-9). Eliphaz is picking up on Zophar's traditional definition of wickedness in terms of social and economic oppression (20:19). But he carries this to a ridiculous extreme in claiming that Job has sinned by hurting his neighbors. This has absolutely no basis in fact; indeed, Eliphaz himself had earlier praised Job's concern for the weak (4:3-4). It appears as if this friend is searching for anything that can make Job repent.

The overall impression is that Eliphaz appears frantic, grasping at straws. He may actually be preaching this last sermon more to himself than to Job. In the face of confused reasoning, the sheer intensity of his words may comfort him.

Job seems remarkably undisturbed by his friend's deterioration. Indeed, he ignores Eliphaz's speech altogether. In chapter 23 he alternates between lamenting and hoping, similar to his speech in chapter 14. This gives way, in 24:1-17, to complaining about God's cold, unjust ways. Job, realizing that nothing his friends are going to say will surprise him, is more concerned with faithfully expressing the cries of his soul. It is as if Eliphaz had never spoken.

In turning to critical considerations, chapter 24 is filled with problems. The first seventeen verses, dealing with the wicked and the oppressed, are difficult to read since they switch subjects without notice. Some think that these verses were jumbled as the book was compiled.

A more serious dilemma arises in the remaining verses of the chapter (24:18-25). It seems impossible for most of this passage to have come from Job's mouth. This section deals mainly with the punishment of the wicked and the corresponding justice of God—a theme vigorously denied by Job in the rest of the book. It is likely that this was a fragment of a friend's speech, inserted here in the editorial process.

Here is an outline of chapters 22-24.

    I. Eliphaz's Third Speech (22:1-30)
      A. Rebuke of Job (22:1-9)
      B. Punishment of the wicked (22:10-20)
      C. Exhortation to Job (22:21-30)
    II. Job's Response (23:1–24:17)
      A. Hope for a court date with God (23:1-17)
      B. Reflection on God's injustice (24:1-17)
   III. Friend's Fragment (24:18-25)

Rebuke of Job (22:1-9)

Eliphaz begins with a two-point insult of Job. First, the suffering Job is worthless in God's eyes, not able to claim anything from the Almighty (verses 2-3). Second, Job is a horrible sinner (verses 4-9). Eliphaz's vehemence suggests the weakening of his argument.

The sense of verse 2 is: Can a mere mortal be useful to God? and, Wise persons are useful only to themselves.

Eliphaz sarcastically asks in verse 4 if Job's pain results from the sufferer's *piety* of the Almighty. This question introduces a new thought, developed in the following verses. It should not be linked to the rhetorical question posed in verse 3.

In verses 6-9 Eliphaz categorizes Job's imagined iniquities in terms of traditional sins (see also 5:15-16; 20:19). For the background of these transgressions, see Exodus 22:21-27, Deuteronomy 24:10-22, and Isaiah 58:7.

A *pledge* (verse 6 NRSV; NIV, *security*) was a piece of personal property given to a creditor as a guarantee that the debt would be paid in the future. Exacting a pledge *for no reason* suggests extortion, where a person is coerced, out of fear, to give a pledge, although there may not be any debt. (See also 17:3; 24:3b, 9b.)

The Punishment of the Wicked (22:10-20)

This standard section in the speeches of the friends contains two noteworthy items. Eliphaz first addresses Job directly, instead of referring to a generic wicked person: *Snares are around you* (verse 10a) and *darkness so that you cannot see* (verse 11a). Second, he offers a doxology (verses 12-14), interrupting his condemnation of Job.

Verses 10-11 rehash the images of the plight of the wicked. Compare them with Bildad's speech in 18:5-11.

The term *heavens* (verse 12) refers to the farthest point from humanity (see the commentary on 11:8).

Verse 13 may be a reference to Job's words in 21:14-15.

The *vaulted heaven* (verse 14 NIV; NRSV, *dome of heaven*), in the ancient view of the world, separated heaven from earth. It corresponds to the *firmament* in the Creation story (see Genesis 1:6-8). It also corresponds to the sky, which is *hard as a molten mirror* (Job 37:18 NRSV; NIV, *mirror cast of bronze*).

Compare verses 15-18 with 21:14-16.

The sense of verse 18 is: God gave them good things, but they were punished by God.

The *adversaries are cut off* (verse 20 NRSV; NIV, *our foes are destroyed*) from abundance and from God.

Exhortation to Job (22:21-30)

Eliphaz's last words follow the traditional *if . . . then* style: If you repent, then God will bless you. The exhortation, in light of his opening comments about God's untouchableness, is not convincing.

In verses 21-23 Eliphaz lists commands, denoting what Job's attitude should be: Agree with God; receive instruction; return to the Almighty; humble yourself; remove unrighteousness.

Like the listing of Job's sins (verses 6-9), the sheer accumulation of such phrases makes them useless. Underneath is Eliphaz's growing uncertainty.

Verse 24: Unless *gold* is meant figuratively, this verse shows again Eliphaz's inability to comprehend Job's situation. Where is Job's gold? Has it not been taken away from him? *Ophir* was a land noted for its abundant gold. Its location is uncertain. (See also 28:16.)

Verses 26-28: As in verses 21-23, the mere listing of such promises underlines the weakness of Eliphaz's argument. Such accumulation is meaningless.

To conclude his confused and contradictory sermon, Eliphaz uses his last tool—a threat (verses 29-30). *Cleanness of your hands* indicates a blameless heart (see 11:13-14).

Hope for a Court Date with God (23:1-7)

Job only indirectly responds to his friend's blustery speech. In verse 2 he states that he will continue being rebellious (a meaning of the Hebrew word translated *bitter*). Rebuffing Eliphaz's pleas for humility, Job affirms a continued rebellion against God's injustice.

In the rest of the chapter, Job vacillates between hoping and doubting. His images are fewer and much more concrete than Eliphaz's. Of special note is that, in the repeat of his wish to see God *in court,* Job does not seek the help of an intermediary. Earlier he had sought an arbitrater (9:33), a *witness* (16:19), and a *Redeemer* (19:25). He had also set conditions that had to be met before confronting the Almighty (13:20-27). Now, though, he appears confident that simply talking to God face to face will be sufficient (verses 4-7).

Some think that *today* (verse 2) shows that the conversation between Job and his friends lasted several days. This could be the third day, corresponding to the third cycle of speeches. The Hebrew has *my hand* instead of *his hand.* Job may be referring to the progression of his disease, now consuming his hand.

Verses 3-7 outline his hope for the court date with God. Note the legal terms: *seat,* (Hebrew; NIV and NRSV, *dwelling) case, arguments, acquitted* (NRSV; NIV, *delivered*), and *judge*. Note also, in regard to the last term, that God may be the judge (7b).

In verses 8-9 Job returns to despairing. He realizes that this God is inaccessible to him. No matter which way he turns, he cannot see the Almighty.

Verses 10-12: Again he dares to hope. His confidence is based on his own righteousness, symbolized by the *way* (or *path*) he has taken (10a, 11b). Like Eliphaz's use of *hand* (22:30), this signifies an inner disposition by an outward form. *Way* is used extensively throughout Job (3:23; 6:18; 13:15; 21:29) to signify one's "walk" in life: does one walk the path of good or evil? (See also Psalm 17:5.)

Regardless of his own righteousness, though, Job realizes that he has no leverage with God (verses 13-14). So he closes the chapter in despair (verses 15-17).

Verse 15: Note how Job shifts easily between ardently seeking God (verse 3) and being *terrified* of the deity.

Verses 16-17: To sum up his depression, Job compiles his favorite images: *heart faint* (17:11), *terrified me* (6:4), *hemmed in* (3:23 NIV, *silenced by*; NRSV, *vanish in*), and *darkness* (19:8).

Reflection on God's Injustice (24:1-17)

Job's preceding despair leads naturally into criticizing God's coldness in relating to humans. As seen in the introduction, the verses here appear jumbled. This outline may make the best sense of them:

Verses 2-4—the acts of the wicked;

Verses 5-12—the plight of the innocent;

Verses 13-17—the murderer, adulterer, thief.

Verse 1 summarizes Job's heresy and sets up the next sixteen verses. The wicked are not judged by God, and the innocent do not receive any divine help.

Remove landmarks (verse 2 NRSV; NIV, *boundary stones*) was an act forbidden in Deuteronomy 19:14. It refers to taking away the land and possessions of another.

Donkey and *ox* (verse 3) signify the entire wealth of the *orphan* and the *widow*. *Pledge* refers to a promise to repay a debt (see the commentary on 22:6).

In verses 5-12 the innocent are categorized as the *hungry* (verses 5-6), the *naked* (verses 7-8, 10) the *fatherless* (NIV; NRSV, *orphan child*) (verse 9), the *thirsty* (verse 11), and the *dying* (verse 12). They are reduced to an animal existence, roaming the *wilderness* (verse 5) and the *mountains* (verse 8).

The wild ass (verse 5) lives far from cities, roaming the wilderness for food (see also 39:5-8).

Verse 9 originally may have appeared after verse 3 or verse 4.

Verse 12 is the point of this section. Just as God does not chastise the wicked, so also God *pays no attention* to the cries of the innocent (NRSV; NIV, *charges no one with wrongdoing*).

The *dark* (14a, 17) and *night* (14b) are friends of the sinners Job names here. Job's friends had said (15:23; 18:18) that such darkness is the punishment of the wicked. Job asserts the opposite.

Friend's Fragment (24:18-25)

As mentioned in the introduction, it is highly unlikely that the bulk of these concluding verses could have come from Job. Some have suggested that they are part of Zophar's third speech. Since all the friends preach God's just punishment of sinners, though, it is impossible to know with certainty whose words these are.

Verses 18-20 are standard images, used by the friends, to convey the plight of the wicked. (See 6:15-18; 8:11-13; 9:25-26.)

Verse 21 seems out of place. It could possibly have followed verse 4.

Verse 25: This word of defiance is more indicative of Job than of one of the friends. It could have been misplaced.

§ § § § § § §

The Message of Job 22–24

Eliphaz's blustery speech is humorous. His arguments, stretched as they are to their absurd limits, provide comic relief. But through that humor the poet subtly slices apart the three friends' traditional theology.

Trying to understand human pain by focusing on God's raw power is absurd. Eliphaz elevates the Almighty to such a point that God appears mysteriously whimsical. No human can affect God one way or the other. God causes everything, the bad as well as the good; the only thing humans can do is merely accept it. God must have a reason behind causing suffering, a reason known only to God.

In giving this simplistic solution, the pillar supporting faith crumbles. We need to know that somehow God is profoundly affected by us. We need to feel that we can in some fashion, change God's thinking and acting. Without the assurance that we are taken seriously by God, our rituals become meaningless and our praying becomes prattling.

Part of our hurt in suffering is believing that God does not care. Job cannot sustain hope because of the fear in the back of his mind that God is distanced from human problems. That is why he perpetually falls into pits of depression. Similarly, in confronting pain we periodically feel as if God has turned a cold heart to us. We don't seem important. Our problems and hurts are meaningless to the Almighty. If only God cared, we wouldn't hurt so much.

Part of our hope lies in trusting that there can be a new, warm relationship with God. Job never gives up. His passion for God sustains him, giving him brief respites from despair: *Oh, that I knew where I might find him, that I might come even to his seat!* Even though despair outweighs hope ten to one in Job, the fire of his brief, passionate surges will ultimately cause a whirlwind encounter with the Lord.

Suffering is suffocating. It can appear that there is no way out. Allowing yourself to believe that there is one who cares deeply for you may be hard to do. But in such times of hoping, you give yourself room to breathe. And you are better prepared when the Lord comes to you in your own whirlwind.

§ § § § § § §

Job 25–27

Introduction to These Chapters

These chapters report the last interchange between Job and the three friends. A poem about wisdom (chapter 28) follows it, before Job finally delivers a long summary monologue (chapters 29–31).

This section is extremely difficult to read because of abrupt, unannounced changes in speakers. Also contributing to the difficulty is the presence of several corrupt and unclear verses. One thing, however, seems evident. Since this is the last exchange between Job and the friends, both sides state things in blunt, emotion-laden terms.

The themes of the friends, for example, are nothing new. They underscore human weakness/divine greatness (25:2-6; 26:5-14), and they rehash the doctrine of the just punishment of the wicked (27:7-23). Their words, though, are concise, with fewer—yet more concrete—images. Bildad illustrates this when he describes human frailty by parodying Psalm 8:4: . . . *How much less man, who is a maggot, and the son of man, who is a worm* (25:6).

For his part, Job spits heavy sarcasm at the "comfort" his friends have given him (26:2-4). He then defiantly concludes by swearing—in God's name—that he will never agree with what his companions have professed (27:2-6). Job says, *I hold fast my righteousness, and will not let it go; my heart does not reproach me for any of my days* (27:6 NRSV).

Two things should be noted about these chapters, critically speaking. First, the only speech we may confidently assign to a specific friend is Bildad's, in 25:2-6. There are two other fragments of speeches that appear to come from the friends: 26:5-14 and 27:7-23. They may be assigned to the friends because they contain themes unique to the comforters. Some have suggested that 26:5-14 may be a continuation of Bildad's third speech (25:2-6). Some have also suggested that 27:7-23 may be part of the missing third speech of Zophar. This is only speculation, though, since there is nothing specified in the text.

It should also be noted that Job's speech is not complete. After initiating a reply to Bildad (26:2-4), it abruptly ends, with the rest of the chapter being a friend's eulogy to God's power. Job resumes in 27:2-6, but it is unclear if this is connected to the earlier speech. As will be seen in the commentary, a debated passage is 27:7-12. It is possible to read these as Job's words as well, but more likely they are from one of the friends.

Why these speeches were so jumbled may never be answered. Perhaps in compiling the book they were accidentally misplaced, or perhaps a pious editor tried to make Job appear more traditional by attributing to him some of his friends' orthodox theology. However it was, this section contains the most problematical chapters in the entire book.

Given these critical problems, here is an outline of chapters 25-27.

    I. Bildad's Third Speech (25:1-6)
   II. Job's Response to Bildad (26:1-4)
  III. Friend's Fragment (26:5-14)
  IV. Job's Fragment (27:1-6)
   V. Friend's Fragment (27:7-23)

Bildad's Third Speech (25:1-6)

Bildad, in his closing words, joins his other friends in contrasting God and humanity. Compare his thoughts here with 4:17-21; 11:5-12; and 15:14-16.

Verse 2 may refer to God's autocratic control over all the angels (or *sons of God*, 1:6; 2:1).

God's *armies* (verse 3 NRSV; NIV, *forces*) are so many that they cannot be counted. This thought connects with Job's experience of God as a powerful *warrior* (16:12-14) and a relentless army commander (19:11-12).

The *moon* and *stars* (verse 5), like angels (4:18), are greater than mere mortals. However, they, too, are *not pure in his* sight.

Job's Response to Bildad (26:1-4)

Using sarcasm to express his anger at his friends is nothing new for Job (see 21:2-3, for example). In this last address to his friends, though, his words are the sharpest and most direct. His sarcasm expresses his deep hurt at the type of "pastoral care" he has received at their hands.

Compare verse 3 with 12:2-3.

In verse 4 Job accuses Bildad of having listened not to God but to an evil spirit.

Friend's Fragment (26:5-14)

The emphasis in this section complements Bildad's discourse on human impotence. The speaker draws a detailed picture of the Almighty's power. He does this by describing God's dominion over key aspects of the ancient view of the world:

> the depths (Sheol)—verses 5-6
> the earth—verse 7
> the clouds—verses 8-9
> the horizon—verse 10
> the mountains—verse 11
> the sea and the serpent—verses 12-13

God's unquestioned control over these works is conveyed through the powerful verbs the speaker uses. God *stretches, binds, covers, stilled,* and *smote.*

Sheol (verses 5-6 NRSV; NIV, *Death*) was the realm of the dead, and *Abbadon* (NRSV; NIV, *Destruction*) was another name for it (see the commentary on 7:9). *Shades* (NRSV; NIV *the dead*) refers to the inhabitants of this underground region. The traditional view was that God had no power in Sheol (see Psalm 88:10-12). Job, accordingly, saw it as a place safe from God's torments (7:9-10). This friend may be stripping Job of this comfort by asserting that Sheol *is naked before God.*

The *north* (verse 7 cf. NIV; NRSV, *Zaphor*) came to be seen as the dwelling place of God (see Isaiah 14:13-14). It may have had its roots in ancient Middle Eastern mythology. The earth, suspended upon *nothing,* baffled the ancient mind, and pointed to the Creator's greatness.

Clouds (verses 8-9) are not only physical but also mystical, as seen in Exodus 13:21-22; 14:19-20. The poet captures the mysteriousness in verse 9; noted that the Hebrew may also mean *throne* rather than *moon.*

Verses 10-11 describe the separation of the heavens from the earth; compare them to Proverbs 8:27-29. *Circle* (NRSV) refers to the *horizon* (NIV), while *pillars* refer to mountains. Mountains were believed to support heaven. The earth, thus, was in the center, between Sheol and heaven.

Verses 12-13 allude to the ancient myth of the deity subduing the *serpent,* also known as *Rahab* and *Leviathan* (see the commentary on 3:8 and on chapter 41). It was only through God's *power* and *understanding* (NRSV; NIV *wisdom*), or craftiness, that such a powerful, chaotic beast could be destroyed. *By his wind* (NRSV; NIV, *breath*) refers to God's blowing away the storm clouds following the battle.

Verse 14: The preceding evidences of God's power are

but a *whisper* compared to the *thunder* of the Almighty's full strength.

Job's Fragment (27:1-6)

Job's last words addressed to his friends are a violent re-affirmation of the one thing that most provoked their animosity. He will never repent of his belief in his own righteousness. God the tormentor is a better friend to Job than these three comforters, who want Job to give up his integrity and profess what he does not believe.

Verse 1 is an unusual introduction to Job's speech; the customary formula is, *Then Job answered* . . . . This preface draws attention to Job's words after the preceding order had been disturbed (see the critical comments in the introduction). Job's speech here follows fragments of other discourses. It is as if an ancient editor noted the interruptions and wanted to call attention back to Job.

Right (verse 2 NRSV) can also be translated *judgment* or *justice* (NIV). A legal term, Job's use of it denotes his conviction that God will not allow a fair trial. It is ironic that even though Job condemns God, he is also swearing by this same deity to assert his own innocence.

Verse 4: There is irony again. Job has the *spirit of the unjust God* (verse 3), yet Job swears he will never *speak falsehood.*

Job has not been convinced by his friends, and would rather die than be comforted by them. He uses the term *integrity* (verse 5) to affirm this. In the prose portion, integrity denoted his refusal to *curse God and die* (2:9). Here, it refers to Job's refusal to admit to something he knows is wrong: that he has sinned and brought suffering on himself.

Heart (verse 6 NRSV) refers to *conscience* (NIV). The heart was the center of the intellect in Hebrew belief (see the commentary on 9:4). Job has a clean conscience.

Friend's Fragment (27:7-23)

This section deals with the fate of the wicked in the traditional manner and thus is unlikely to have come from Job. These verses are so jumbled that a clear understanding is difficult, if not impossible.

As noted in the introduction, some attribute verses 7-8 to Job. From that perspective, the sense is that Job is comparing his friends to the *wicked*, ironically twisting their own terminology. More likely, though, a comforter is speaking to Job. It is one of the most biting of all addresses: Job is no longer a friend but an *enemy*, given up to the ranks of the *godless*.

Verses 9-10: The friend is explaining to Job why the sufferer feels so lonely. God does not answer the prayers of the wicked.

Verses 11-12 appear out of place in this section. They may be part of another speech, perhaps by Job, the rest of which is lost. The *you* is in the plural, suggesting that Job is addressing the three men. He is accusing them of theological ignorance. He also accuses them of being *vain*, a vanity that has shut their ears to reason. It is possible, however, to believe that one of the friends may be addressing Job and the other companions; Bildad started his second speech in this fashion (18:2). The friend may be exhorting Job to listen one last time.

Verses 13-23 contain the losses the wicked person will experience. Such a sinner will be deprived of: a future (verses 13-15), wealth (verses 16-19), and emotional stability (verses 20-23).

The style of verse 13 is quite similar to Zophar's. Compare this with 20:29.

Verse 15b: Grieving, in the ancient world, was an affirmation of the deceased person's life. For there to be no *mourning* at a funeral, thus, is an insult.

Job describes himself as *just* in 12:4 and as *innocent* in 9:23. The friend, in this "the meek shall inherit the earth" verse (verse 17), thus turns the tables on Job. Job is actually the wicked person.

The *booth* (verse 18 NRSV; NIV, *hut*) of a watchman, or guard, was where he kept watch and/or took shelter. It was a small, temporary, and very flimsy construction.

Compare verse 20 with Bildad's words in 18:11-14.

East wind (verse 21) refers to a hot, destructive desert wind. (See the commentary on 15:2.)

Verses 22-23: *It* refers to the east wind, but is also synonymous with God's harsh punishment of the wicked. *Claps its hands*—To clap hands at someone was a form of contempt (see Lamentations 2:15; Ezekiel 25:6).
Hisses—Similar to clapping, this was an act of derision (see Lamentations 2:15-16; Ezekiel 27:36; Zephaniah 2:15).

§ § § § § § §

The Message of Job 25–27

Progressively, the friends have grown more abrasive as they have attempted to justify their theology. Bildad's lofty depiction of God, and the accompanying degradation of humanity, is a poignant example. The intent is to argue, not to comfort.

Such insensitivity underscores the fact that the sufferer needs to know that he or she is important. Job wants to be respected for his thoughts and struggles. Behind this is his need to know that somehow his pain really does make a difference, that it does matter to somebody. To die slowly, believing that such death is natural and inconsequential, is perhaps worse than the physical pain.

The sufferer faces life "sarcastically" when he or she is degraded. Sarcasm allows a person to voice anger while laughing at the absurdity of the world. Reading Job's hot, sarcastic reply to Bildad, one can almost sense Job's bitter laughter. Such laughter is his way of putting his companions in their place. It is his way of saying that he does not deserve the harsh treatment inflicted upon him.

Behind the sarcasm is an affirmation of integrity. His friends' constant debating does not soften Job. On the contrary, it makes him see his own situation more clearly. He does not have the answers as to why he is suffering. He is only sure that he has done nothing to warrant it. This surety grows in him and gives rise to his powerful proclamation of innocence in 27:2-6.

Such integrity is perhaps our only light while going through the darkest night. It takes strength to say, with Job, *Till I die, I will not put away my integrity from me* (NRSV; NIV, *I will not deny . . .*; 27:5*b*). In the very act of saying that, though, we have given God an open invitation.

§ § § § § § §

Job 28

Introduction to This Chapter

Chapter 28, upon first reading, seems out of place. It completely interrupts the drama that has been unfolding in the prior twenty-seven chapters. It does not advance the dialogue between Job and his friends, nor does it promote Job's summary speech that follows (chapter 29-31).

The poet probably intended it this way, however. He has inserted an "aside," a brief rest from the intense, heated dialogue.

This intermission takes the form of a beautifully mysterious twenty-eight verse poem reflecting on *wisdom*. As seen in the Introduction (see "How the Book Was Written"), seeking wisdom refers to seeking to understand the mysteries of the world. Because of the problem of unexplained suffering, this takes a special twist in the book of Job. Here wisdom refers to understanding God's interaction with humans and discerning our proper response.

The poet, in chapter 28, takes an extremely pessimistic view regarding this subject. Job's friends have appeared foolish in their clumsy attempts at explaining, in traditional theological terms, Job's suffering. The poet explains their buffoonery. After praising human ingenuity in the opening verses, he asks if humans can also be ingenious in understanding life's perplexities (that is, pain). The poet answers with an emphatic no: *Mortals* do not *know the way to it* (NRSV; NIV *comprehend its worth)* [such wisdom], *and it is not found in the land of the living* (28:13).

Such a statement serves to let us know—if we have not already guessed—where the poet stands in the debate between Job and the three men. The friends, thinking they are wise, are theologically bankrupt. Job, though, is seeking the source of wisdom: God. *God understands the way to it* [wisdom], *and he knows its place* (28:23 NRSV; NIV, *he alone knows where it dwells*).

Because he does not have answers, and because he is seeking to ask God questions, Job is actually the wise man!

It is important to make two additional observations. First, this chapter reflects the "international" flavor of the book, and can best be understood against the backdrop of the entire ancient Middle Eastern world. As has been noted earlier in several places (see 3:8; 7:12; 26:12-13), the poet alludes to myths and legends that originated in lands outside Palestine. Now, in chapter 28, he refers to mining technology and materials alien to Hebrew culture. Silver, gold, copper, and sapphires, for example, were found in other places in Mesopotamia—such as in the mines of Egypt.

Second, this poem should not be viewed as part of a speech by Job. The character of these verses is cool, restrained, dispassionate. Job's speeches, on the other hand, soar to the heights of hope or drop to the depths of despair; they brim with emotion. Moreover, even though the sentiments of chapter 28 are not alien to Job's views, they are not the same, either. Indeed, the chapter contains striking similarities to the Lord's speeches from the whirlwind (chapters 38–41). It is best, all things considered, to view chapter 28 as a direct statement to us by the poet. It is the only place in the book where we can hear his words directly.

Here is an outline of chapter 28.

   I. Human Ingenuity Regarding Treasures (28:1-11)
   II. Human Limitations Regarding Wisdom (28:12-22)
   III. God's Supremacy (28:23-28)

Human Ingenuity Regarding Treasures (28:1-11)

This section affords us a glimpse into what was important to the ancient world. Not only were silver, gold, and gems valuable—as they are today—but also treasured were the mundane metals of iron and copper. The latter materials were essential for armament and construction.

These verses also celebrate human craftiness. When such valuables are close to their grasp, people employ intricate, creative, and sometimes hazardous measures. The mining methods described here were considered "high tech" in the ancient world. It was their equivalent to our computer-generated technology.

Miners put an end to darkness (verse 3) refers to the artificial light used by miners. *To the farthest recesses* means that the miners go to the very bottom of the earth, touching the boundaries of the mysterious Sheol (see the commentary on 7:95). This is a very risky, scary undertaking, as underscored by the concluding phrase in the verse: *gloom and deep darkness* (NRSV), or *the blackest darkness* (NIV). The King James Version pointedly translates this, *darkness and the shadow of death.*

Verse 4 emphasizes again the dangers risked by the miners. There is an isolation in their work; they could, thus, face peril away from human help. There is also a precariousness in their methods: far from civilization, they swing to and fro. This may refer to being suspended by ropes in the darkness of the mine shafts.

Verse 5 contrasts what is produced on the earth's surface with what is produced underneath. *Turned up as by fire* acknowledges that precious metals and stones were forged by the fires smoldering in the earth's depths. Possibly this idea came from knowledge of volcanoes and of the smelting process.

That path (verse 7) refers to the depths of the earth. Birds and animals possess keen eyesight and strength. They are well equipped to explore and rule the wilderness. Only humans, though, can plumb the earth's bowels.

Verses 9-11 celebrate the actual construction of mines. They build up human ingenuity to grandiose proportions, preparing for the description of human limitation in the next section.

Overturns mountains by the roots (NRSV; NIV, *lays bare the roots of mountains*) means that miners undercut the strength of the mighty mountains by digging beneath them.

Channels are mineshafts. By sinking such shafts, *every precious thing*—concealed and guarded by the earth—is seen by human eye. The act of seeing something suggests the ability to obtain or control it, a thought echoed in verses 21 and 24.

Searching for the source of rivers (verse 11) refers to the underground caves which the miners explored. In mythology, such underground rivers were the domain of El, the father of the gods. This again suggests the bravery of the miners in entering the eerie, dark, watery realm.

Human Limitations of Wisdom (28:12-22)

Abruptly this praise is interrupted by the question, *But where shall wisdom be found?* (verse 12). Humans know where earthly treasures are stored, and can grasp them through their cunning. But they do not even have the slightest idea where wisdom is, least of all how to go about "mining" it.

The question in verse 12 serves as the turning point in the chapter. Asking a question, then philosophizing, was a technique of the Hebrew wise men (see Proverbs 23:29-30; Ecclesiastes 8:1). Note also that *wisdom* and *understanding* are used synonymously, another characteristic in their writing style (Proverbs 1:2; 4:5, 7).

It is not *found in the land of the living* (verse 13) puts wisdom completely beyond human reach.

Deep and *sea* (verse 14) are synonymous. They may

refer to the world's oceans, seen as rising from underground. Note that they are personified, perhaps suggesting their mythological character (see the commentary on verse 11*a*).

Verses 15-19: By extensively listing earthly treasures, the poet is showing, by comparison, how priceless wisdom is. With the exception of verse 18, *gold* is used repeatedly as the standard of great value.

Ophir (verse 16) was a land, of uncertain location, known in the ancient world for its abundant *gold* (see 22:24).

Glass (verse 17 NRSV; NIV, *crystal*) was a valuable commodity, used with *gold* to form jewelry.

Ethiopia (verse 19) designates a territory south of Egypt.

Verses 20-22 repeat, in form, verses 12-14. Such repetition emphasizes the theme of the section: Wisdom is totally inaccessible.

Verse 20 is identical to verse 12 with the exception of *then*. This change denotes the conclusion the poet draws after the prior listing of wealth.

Verse 21 repeats verse 13 insofar as wisdom is not in the realm of the *living*. The poet adds the image of the sharp eyes of birds, as he mentioned in verse 7.

Personification is used again in verse 22, as in verse 14. This time, the realm of the dead is queried regarding wisdom. *Abaddon* (NRSV; NIV, *Death*) is another name for Sheol, where the dead dwelt; see the commentary on 7:9. The response of this domain (v. 22*b*) suggests that the dead are closer to obtaining understanding than are the living.

God's Supremacy (28:23-28)

Human limitations form the backdrop for praise of God. Although people may have dominion over the earth, and can even discover treasure under the earth. God alone controls the one thing untouchable by human hand. The Almighty knows and controls those things which, to people, appear as the mysteries of life.

To describe this "otherness" of God, the poet praises God's control over creation. The description of this control bears similarities to the Lord's speech in chapter 38.

Verse 23 answers the question posed in verses 12 and 20. God's understanding surpasses all human technology.

Verse 24: The miner goes *to the ends of the earth* (see verse 3), and the falcon *sees everything under the heavens* (see verse 7). God, however, does both these things, and does them in ways beyond human comprehension.

Verses 25-27 associate wisdom with the act of Creation. This was a popular concept among the Hebrew wise men (see Proverbs 3:19-20).

Note that the description of how God creates in verses 25-26 is given in technical, almost "miner-like" terminology.

It (verse 27) refers to wisdom. After the act of Creation—perhaps because of it—wisdom became a part of God. The powerful verbs used underscore the Almighty's dominion over such understanding. God creates, shapes, and refines wisdom.

Many believe verse 28 to be an addition to the poem by a later editor. *And he said* . . . is an abrupt intrusion. Also, a special Hebrew term for Lord is used—*Adonai*. Used only here, it is a reverent term, in contrast to the more generic word translated *God* throughout Job. However, the tenor of the verse is in keeping with the overall thrust of the book. True wisdom for humans begins with the proper attitude: *the fear of the Lord*. This stance of humility before God has been a theme throughout Eliphaz's speeches (4:6; 15:4; 22:4). It was also a formula used by Hebrew sages (see Psalm 111:10; Proverbs 1:7; 3:7; 9:10).

§ § § § § § §

The Message of Job 28

What is *wisdom* for us? This chapter reveals that it is not something that can be attained. It is not arriving at answers, as Job's friends vainly attempted. Rather, it is an ongoing process of asking questions. These are questions at the jagged edge of our faith. They are the queries that cannot be resolved, that agitate us and perhaps make us uncomfortable with our religious certainties. "How can I relate to God when nothing makes sense anymore?" "Where can I find God when the world looks so cold and lonely?" "How can I believe in God when there doesn't appear to be any future for me?"

Accept your limitations. Doubtless the ancient wise men thought they could discover anything if they sufficiently contemplated the world around them through the eyes of philosophy. The image of miners seeking treasures may have been symbolic of this. Our technology seduces us into a similar line of thought. All we need is the right data for the computer. Both the ancient and modern minds are wrong. We are vulnerable to life experiences that will make us question our answers and force us to ask unanswerable questions. To acknowledge this limitation, opens us to life in a new way.

Allow the answers to come from God. Atheists are people who confront life-wrenching questions and respond that God cannot exist. Job-like people encounter the same questions and affirm that answers rest ultimately with the Creator. Those answers are not given in trite, simplistic phrases. Rather, they bypass the mind. The Spirit touches our spirits. Hearts discover the Presence, that produces an unexplainable calm.

§ § § § § § §

PART TWELVE Job 29–31

Introduction to These Chapters

God is on trial for alleged abuse of power, such as in causing the innocent to suffer and allowing the wicked to go free. Job is the prosecuting attorney; his speech in chapter 3 is the opening statement by the prosecution. God's defense attorneys are Job's three friends. With the exception of the preceding chapter, the book of Job has so far occupied itself with presenting arguments between these two sides.

Completing this analogy, chapters 29-31 are the closing statements for the prosecution. Like a skilled lawyer making a final speech before a jury, Job—in carefully summarizing his argument—deftly laces emotion with reason.

He presses two points. First, God has callously and maliciously abused him. In chapter 29 he paints a beautiful, almost idyllic picture of the intimate relationship the Lord and Job once shared. In the following chapter he then shows how, without any provocation whatsoever, God turned on him. This same God changed into an enemy. Reading these two passages, one is touched by Job's deep hurt at this betrayal by God, his closest friend.

Second, Job is careful to prove, beyond any shadow of doubt, that he has done nothing to cause this vicious treatment. It was mentioned in the prose section (1:1-5) that Job was vigilant in his piety, careful never to sin. Throughout his debate with his friends, furthermore, he claimed innocence (see 23:1-7; 27:5-6). Now, in chapter 31, he goes one step further. Claiming to have led a spotless life, he meticulously—and somewhat tediously—reviews several different ways of sinning. He states unequivocally that he is blameless in each respect.

Critically speaking, the biggest problem these chapters offer is that of seemingly misplaced verses. For example: 29:21-25 should possibly follow 29:10; 31:38-40 should probably be read earlier in chapter 31. Such portions make for difficult reading.

This speech closes the dialogue section of the book. Following Elihu's discourses (chapters 32–37), Job's closing arguments will be answered by God.

Here is an outline of chapters 29–31.
   I. Job's Past Happiness (29:1-25)
  II. Job's Present Suffering (30:1-31)
 III. Job's Oath of Innocence (31:1-34)
  IV. Job's Challenge to God (31:35-37)
   V. Renewal of Job's Innocence (31:38-40)

Job's Past Happiness (29:1-25)

This passage is one of the most touching found in the Bible. Amid his physical and emotional problems, Job nostalgically recalls the life he once enjoyed (29:1). Focal to that life was the friendship and protection of God. Due to that relationship, Job enjoyed immense respect in society.

The order of this chapter is forcefully simple:
•recalling God's blessings (verses 2-6);
•recalling society's respect (verses 7-10);
•recalling his acts of kindness (verses 11-20);
•recalling again society's respect (verses 21-25)

Verse 1 is the same unusual introduction found in 27:1. This editorial comment indicates a disorder in the preceding text and the beginning of a new section.

Verses 2-6: The result of God's friendship was Job's experience of divine protection from evil and harm.

Darkness, for Job, carries the meaning of lurking, threatening danger (see 17:12-16).

My prime (verse 4) is, in Hebrew, *autumn days,* the fruitful time of the year when harvests are gathered. Job, consequently, is referring not to the twilight of life but rather to that period which was the happiest for him. *Tent* (NRSV; NIV, *house*) symbolizes a person's life (see 5:24-25). God's *friendship* in that regard signifies safety and prosperity.

Clearly, Job's *children* (verse 5) are utmost in his mind as an indication of divine friendship and protection.

One's *path* (verse 6; NIV; NRSV, *steps*) refers to Job's life (see 14:16). *Milk* (NRSV; NIV, *cream*) and *oil* symbolize prosperity. They are similar to the Exodus phrase of *a land flowing with milk and honey* (Exodus 3:8, 17).

Perhaps because of God's favor, Job was highly respected by all. He was accorded status equal to that of nobility (verse 9). People did not interrupt him, and they sought his advice.

A *gate* (verse 7) was the entrance to the city. *Square* was the center of the city, where business and legal proceedings occurred. By combining gate and square in one verse, Job says that he was respected wherever he went.

Verses 11-20: The acts of compassion noted here reinforce his status in society. They also refute Eliphaz's trumped up allegations of Job's wickedness (22:6-9). The essence of righteousness is helping those who are weak or in special need: the *poor, fatherless* (NIV; NRSV, *orphan*), *widow, blind,* and *lame.*

Verse 12b: In Hebrew society, when the father died, and if there were no other adult male relatives, the children were helpless.

Instead of keeping his distance, Job comforted the dying (verse 13). The *widow,* without the protection of a husband, was especially vulnerable in society. This continued into New Testament times (Mark 12:38-44; Acts 6:1).

Verse 14: Comparing virtues to putting on clothing was a popular image (see Isaiah 59:17).

Verse 16 refers to a stranger. Strangers in a foreign land were also vulnerable, needing special protection (Exodus 22:21).

Compare verse 17 with 4:10. The helpless were devoured by the ruthless as an animal devours defenseless prey. Job stood on the side of the weak, confronting society's lions.

As a result of his righteousness, Job expected to be rewarded with long life (verse 18), children (verse 19), and health (verse 20). Note especially the image of *roots* in earlier usage (8:16-17; 14:7-9; 18:16).

Verses 21-25: Some suggest, quite logically, that this section should follow verses 7-10, since both deal with society's admiration of Job. However, Job's repeat of the respect once given him may simply indicate how much it means to him and how much he misses it.

Job's words encouraged new life in his listeners, just as *spring rain* (verse 23) helps seeds take root and sprout (see Deuteronomy 32:2).

Verse 24: See Proverbs 16:15, which ties together a king's *countenance* (NRSV), or *face* (NIV), with the beneficial effect of rain.

Job's Present Suffering (30:1-31)

This section harshly grates against the preceding picture. The *but now* in verse 1 is a warning that what follows contrasts sharply with Job's peaceful past. His present suffering breaks down into three categories:

- •social pain (verses 1-15);
- •physical pain (verse 16-19);
- •spiritual pain (verses 20-31)

Given the preceding section, Job appropriately begins the listing of his woes by describing his loss of social status. The first eight verses describe society's outcasts. This description is similar to that in 24:5-12. There is a difference, though, in that here the outcasts are seen in an angry light. Job, who had repeatedly aided them, is perhaps disturbed that they have not helped him in his time of need. The only gratitude he gets from them is derision (verses 9-15).

Younger men (verse 1) showing no respect to an older person was a cruel insult. *Dogs* were dishonored in Jewish society (2 Samuel 16:9; 2 Kings 8:13; Matthew 15:26). To call a person's father unworthy to sit with sheepdogs was extremely offensive.

Verse 2: These outcasts were profitless to employers. This was due perhaps to their untrustworthiness (see verse 5) as well as to their overall weakness. There is no hint of compassion for such people, who have now turned against Job.

Mallow (verse 4 NRSV; NIV, *salt herbs*), a tasteless, soft plant, was food for the poor. It grew in the wilderness outside the city limits. The *broom* tree (see 1 Kings 19:4-5) was a desert bush burned for warmth by wandering outcasts.

Nettles (verse 7 NRSV; NIV, *brush*) refers to a type of thorny bush or large, prickly weed (see also Proverbs 24:31).

Note that the *and now* (verse 9), as in verses 1 and 16, emphasizes Job's plight in the present.

Verse 10: As today, spitting was an act of contempt (see Isaiah 50:6).

The image in verse 14 is that of a *breach* in the protective wall of a city. Invaders entered through such an opening. (See also 16:14).

Verse 15: The Hebrew word translated *terrors* means *those things which wear down and destroy. Honor* and *prosperity* (NRSV; NIV, *dignity* and *safety*) are interchangeable here; if a person lost prosperity, as Job did, then the person also lost respect in the eyes of society.

In describing his physical pain one last time, Job incorporates several key images he used in earlier laments.

Verse 17: His inability to rest is caused by the sores covering his entire body (see 2:7).

Verse 18: God may be seen as the subject of this verse, tying it to verse 19. Job is thus saying that God has grabbed him and thrown him down. Contrast this to his earlier recollection of God's friendship (29:2-4).

Verses 20-23: As in 13:13–14:22, Job interrupts his thoughts with this four-verse "aside" speech to God. Here he directly accuses the Lord of cruelty; compare his accusations here with his earlier ones (7:20-21; 9:13-35; 19:6-20). In the remainder of the chapter Job returns to lamenting his pain, thus illustrating this viciousness.

I cry . . . I stand. . . (verse 20): Job is desperately trying to get God's attention, but to no avail.

The image in verse 22 is that of being buffeted by a violent storm, while having nothing to grasp.

Verse 26 is a brutal confrontation of the friends' pious belief that good people will be rewarded. Job had done good to others, but when he *expected good* he received nothing but *evil.*

Verse 27 refers to conscience (see 9:4). Job is bombarded by disturbing thoughts.

Although *blackened* (verse 28 NIV) may refer to Job's skin disease, it also conveys a sense of depression: "*I go about in sunless gloom* (NRSV), even during the day."

Jackals and *ostriches* (verse 29 NRSV; NIV *owls*) are animals of the wilderness or desert, far from the city.

Verse 31 is sarcastic. The *pipe* and *lyre* (NRSV; NIV, *flute* and *harp*), instruments of praise (Psalm 33:2), are used by Job to mourn what the Lord has done to him.

Job's Oath of Innocence (31:1-34)

Job goes through examples of sin, exonerating himself in each one. There are sixteen of these, each beginning with *if* (verses 5, 7, 9, 13, 16, 19, 20, 21, 24, 25, 26, 29, 31, 33, 38, 39). Some of these are accompanied by a curse. Numbers 5:11-22 somewhat parallels this style.

Verse 1 sets the tone for the rest of the chapter. Job will not even entertain thoughts that could lead to sin.

Verses 2-4: Job, perhaps sarcastically, restates the traditional belief of divine punishment/reward. He will show himself, in this chapter, to be immaculate in terms of traditional righteousness. Thus, if the view that God punishes the wicked and blesses the pure is true, Job asserts that God must have made a mistake in his case.

The images in verse 7 depict greed and lust. They follow the ancient form of using physical items to symbolize spiritual states. Dirty *hands,* for example, point to having committed a sinful action.

Grind (verse 10) may refer to his wife working for someone, such as by grinding in a mill. It may also have sexual connotations, in keeping with the rest of the verse.

Abaddon (verse 12 NRSV; NIV, *Destruction*) is another name for Sheol, where the dead dwelt (see the commentary on 7:9).

Verse 13: Such servants were to be treated justly (see Jeremiah 34:8-22).

Verse 14 may refer to God's judging action (see Numbers 10:35).

Note the radical concept of equality in verse 15.

The *eyes of the widow* (verse 16) could *fail* (NRSV; NIV, *grow weary*) either by weeping or by looking for food.

The sin in verse 17 is in eating alone, not sharing food with the starving fatherless.

The meaning of verse 18 is that Job had a close relationship with the poor and weak.

Verse 21: It would be a sin for Job to join others *(help in the gate)* in striking a defenseless person.

Verse 22: The curse for striking the weak was the destruction of the offending bodily part, such as the arm. Jesus used this theme in Matthew 5:29-30.

Verses 26-27 refer to the idolatry of worshiping the *sun* and *moon,* a popular pagan custom (2 Kings 23:5). Verse 27b describes an ancient form of adoration (1 Kings 19:18).

Verse 29: Contrast Job's high ethical standards to the sentiments in Psalms 9 and 10.

Verses 31-32: See the commentary on 29:16b. Verse 31 speaks of Job's fellow clansmen.

Job's Challenge to God (31:35-37)

Job, having exonerated himself, now casts the burden of proof onto God. Job is innocent of any crime; is God? The sufferer challenges the Almighty to prove that innocence in court. Such a challenge is not new (see 9:33; 13:3; 19:25). However, here in his closing words the challenge is presented in its clearest, most direct form.

Putting one's name on a document (verse 35) signified the seriousness of the signer (see Colossians 4:18). In Job's case, this has the flavor of signing a legal document in court, validating his case.

Verse 37: If these are his last words—if verses 38-40 belong elsewhere—then Job is ending on anything but a humble note. He has made his case, he has challenged God, and, if God responds, Job will appear in the courtroom *like a prince.*

Renewal of Job's Innocence (31:38-40)

These verses probably belong in the earlier portion of chapter 31, where Job is examining and proclaiming his righteousness. The sin postulated in this section is that of obtaining land in unjust ways, such as through killing the landowner. A concrete example is the story of Naboth's vineyard (1 Kings 21). Note the personification of *land;* compare this to Job's earlier use (16:18; see also Genesis 4:10).

§ § § § § § §

The Message of Job 29–31

Living "the good life" does not mean God is blessing us.
Job, in recalling his happy past, equates God's friendship
with status in society and protection from harm.
Similarly, when we find things happily prosperous, we
consider such fortune a nice sign from God.

Because Job encounters suffering, though, does not
mean that God has abandoned him. On the contrary, it is
precisely Job's righteousness that brings on his pain.
Likewise, losing what once was fulfilling to us does not
mean we have lost favor with God. Rather, it means that
our relationship with the Lord is entering a new phase, a
phase of challenge and perhaps growth.

*Certainty of our righteousness enables us to confront
suffering.* The exhaustiveness of chapter 31 shows how
important this is for Job. Knowing that he has done
nothing to bring on his pain is vital to him. Once he is
assured of that, he opens his heart to God, talking to the
Almighty in honest, angry, blunt terms.

We need not be as exhaustive as Job. Christ has shown
us the reality of grace. Knowing we are forgiven frees us
to talk to God openly. The first thing we can ask is, "God,
if I have not done anything to deserve this pain, then
why am I seemingly being punished?"

Getting God's attention opens the door for God's entrance.
Job knocks loudly when he lays down his challenge for a
court date. As seen in the closing chapters of the book,
this draws the Lord into a whirlwind appearance.

How do we get God's attention? Perhaps by crying
over the injustice of a situation. Perhaps by whispering
prayers of angry desperation in the middle of the night.
Perhaps by daring God as boldly as Job does.

§ § § § § § §

Job 32–34

Introduction to These Chapters

The section of Job covered by Parts 13 and 14 (chapters 32-37) surprises us. It is natural to assume that, following Job's fiery challenge to God in chapter 31, we would find the Lord's reply. That response is delayed, however. Instead, a brash young man named Elihu explodes upon the scene.

His appearance is explained in chapter 32. He is the youngest of the men with Job, so it is proper that he speak last. The reason he speaks at all is that Job's friends have done such a bad job in dealing with the sufferer. Job is still proclaiming his righteousness, so it is up to Elihu to set him straight.

If one word describes his character, it is "arrogance." To him, things are right or wrong, cut and dried. Consequently, filled with the angry idealism of youth, he spits out sentences in rapid, machine gun-like fashion. He is confident that if Job and the three friends are sufficiently bombarded by his insights, then things will be resolved.

Such haughtiness broods just under the surface of his two opening speeches, chapters 33 and 34. He turns first to Job (chapter 33). In a condescending manner, he tells Job the error of his ways: God is speaking to the sufferer through the suffering, so Job should be quiet and listen. He next turns to the three friends (chapter 34). In an equally condescending tone, he criticizes their inability to silence Job. He also preaches a homily to them concerning God's unfathomable justice—as if they had never heard of it.

The other side of arrogance is anger, and it is possible to see Elihu's righteous indignation building to a boiling point in the short span of these two speeches. He addresses Job courteously enough in the opening verses of chapter 33. However, by the end of his second address his temper has gotten the best of him. Talking to the friends, he states: *Would that Job were tried to the limit, because his answers are those of the wicked!* (34:36 NRSV). Job's three companions never gave him a drop of comfort. Elihu will give even less.

Critically speaking, most scholars think that these chapters were penned by someone other than the poet who wrote the rest of the book. There are many reasons for this. One has already been seen, namely, that the Elihu section seems to intrude upon the action already taking place. Another factor is that the language in these chapters is often different from the rest of Job. Terms in Aramean, a dialect similar to Hebrew, punctuate this fourth friend's addresses. Perhaps most convincing of all, Elihu is never mentioned elsewhere in Job. He is conspicuously absent when the others are introduced (2:11). He is also omitted in the epilogue (42:7-9), when Job's friends are ordered to repent.

It is probably best to see the character of Elihu as an attempt by later generations to answer Job's blasphemies. Elihu is the spokesman for Jewish orthodoxy, the view upholding the doctrine of divine rewarding of the good and punishing of the bad.

Here is an outline of chapters 32–34.
  I. Introduction of Elihu (32:1-5)
 II. Elihu's Poetic Introduction (32:6-22)
III. Elihu's First Speech (33:1-33)
    A. Invitation to Job (33:1-7)
    B. Job's sin (33:8-11)

Introduction of Elihu (32:1-5)

This introduction explains Elihu's appearance in terms of the friends' failure to silence the righteous Job. It also tells us his mood. The adjective *angry* appears four times in this short section.

The name *Elihu* means *My God is he.* It was a popular Hebrew name (see 1 Samuel 1:1; 1 Chronicles 12:20; 26:7; 27:18). *Barachel,* his father, stands for *God has blessed. Buzite* refers to someone from Buz, an Arabian tribe or territory. *Ram* is the name of the clan to which Elihu belonged; ancient Middle Eastern extended families were designated by a chief male whose name identified them.

Elihu's Poetic Introduction (32:6-22)

Elihu himself gives reasons for his intervention. In his opening words he lists three of these. He speaks due to:
- the insights revealed to him by God (verses 6-10);
- the failure of Job's three friends (verses 11-16);
- his own enthusiasm (verses 17-22).

These opening sremarks also betray Elihu's self-consciousness. He admits feeling timid, fearful to speak because of his youth (verse 6). Also, he repeatedly refers to himself in the first person, describing the depth of his character and the sincerity of his feelings. The self-consciousness continues into his first two speeches, where he asks his hearers several times to *listen* to him. Such nervousness perhaps points to the feeling of the later writer who inserted the Elihu section into the book.

The images in verse 7 are allusions to Job's three friends, who are older than Elihu.

Spirit (verse 8), in Hebrew, also means *wind*. This explains its similarity to the phrase that follows, *the breath of the Almighty.* Eliphaz (4:12-19) and Job (27:3-4) also claim divine inspiration.

In verses 11-16, Elihu is addressing Job's three companions. Job's friends cannot leave it up to God to repudiate Job. Elihu will not follow the line of thought advanced by Job's friends. He will, rather, answer Job with new ideas.

Verse 19: New wine must have room for expansion, or it will burst its container. Jesus used this image in Matthew 9:17.

Not showing *partiality* (verse 21) is a sign of truthfulness. Elihu warns that he will not show the compassionate restraint (as if there were any) to Job that the three friends did.

Invitation to Job (33:1-7)

Courteously, Elihu invites Job to enter a dialogue with him (verses 5-7). He prefaces this request, however, by carefully asserting his authority (verses 1-4). The impression is that Elihu is too eager to speak to desire a real dialogue with the sufferer.

Elihu follows the ancient technique of using physical things *(words, lips)* to signify an inner disposition. *Heart* (verse 3) refers to the conscience (see the commentary on 9:4).

Spirit of God (verse 4) is a recurring theme for Elihu (see 32:8, 18). Believing himself to possess *the breath of the Almighty,* he is eager to speak for God.

Verses 5-7: This courteous invitation to Job is humorous. First, he invites Job to *answer* him, but this comes after Elihu has claimed to speak for God. Who would dare respond? Second, he says that he will not put pressure upon Job, intimidating him. But who would not be intimidated by this angry, arrogant young theologian?

Job's Sin (33:8-11)

Describing Job's wickedness sets up the main part of his speech, which follows in the next section. Job's impudence will require a theological reply.

Elihu hears only Job's *words* (verse 8). He chooses not to relate, or is incapable of relating, to the sufferer on a feeling level.

Elihu compiles these verses from Job's earlier speeches: verse 9 (9:21; 10:7*a*); verse 10 (13:24); verse 11 (13:27). He claims that Job's guilt lies in professing never to have sinned. Job, however, has conceded the possibility of transgression (7:21; 13:26). The sufferer simply contends that whatever he may have done does not merit the severity of his pain.

God's Saving Actions (33:12-30)

God saves, according to Elihu, by helping people see their sin and repent. God speaks in two ways: dreams (verses 15-18) and pain (verses 19-30). Elihu also adds a new concept. To aid in teaching the sufferer, God employs a *mediator* (verses 23-30).

In verse 13, he misquotes Job's words in 23:5.

One way and in two (verse 14, NRSV; NIV, *now one way, now another*) is a dramatic manner of saying, "two ways." (See other examples of this in 5:19 and Psalm 62:11.) The *one* who does *not perceive* God's words is Job.

Compare verse 15 to Eliphaz's night vision (4:12-17). For another example of the Hebrew understanding of revelation through dreams, see Numbers 12:6-8.

Verse 18: Note Elihu's prolific use of the term *Pit:* verses 22*a*, 24*a*, 28, 30. It symbolizes death and the grave (see also 17:14; Psalms 30:9; 94:13).

The mediator is not one who would justify the sufferer in a heavenly court, as Job desires (see 16:19). Rather, according to Elihu, such a spiritual being would tell Job what he should do, and then ask God to bless Job—after the sufferer repents.

One of a thousand (verse 23) refers to the large size of the heavenly beings—*angels*—surrounding God. This number should not be taken literally.

Ransom (verse 24) carries the meaning of covering something in order to appease (see Exodus 21:30). Here it refers to something given to make the Almighty forgive, or cover, a person's sins.

It was a Hebrew custom (see Psalm 22:22-31) to praise God following an answered prayer (verses 26-28).

Twice, three times (verse 29) means *several times*. This manner of speaking is similar to verse 14.

Admonition to Job (33:31-33)

Intentionally or not, Elihu ends on a humorous note. He tells Job to be quiet (verse 31), then encourages him to speak (verse 32), and then again orders silence (verse 33). The final impression is that of a young man thoroughly caught up in what he is saying—and perhaps a bit unsure. Elihu's overriding concern, though, is evident in verse 31: *Pay attention, Job, listen to me* . . . .

Job's Arrogance (34:1-9)

In this second speech, Elihu addresses the three friends. As he taught God's ways to Job, so will he admonish them. He begins, though, by once again condemning Job. It is as if he cannot let loose of his anger against the rebellious sufferer.

Wise men (verse 2) is a sarcastic reference to Job's three friends. Elihu considers them anything but wise, since they were unable to silence Job (see 32:9).

Verse 3 is a proverbial saying, similar to 12:11.

Compare verses 5-6 to 9:20-21; 27:2*a*.

Keeping *company with evildoers* (verse 8) was viewed as proof of a person's sinfulness (see 22:15; Psalm 1:1). Note

Job's words in 30:1-14, however: The *wicked* men are not friends but persecuters.

Verse 9 is a good summary of Job's views in 21:7-16.

God's Impartiality (34:10-30)

The friends, according to Elihu, should better understand the greatness of God's justice. He passionately preaches this; as in his speech to Job (33:1, 31, 33), he orders his listeners to pay close attention to such an insight (verses 10, 16).

There is irony here. The three friends have repeatedly lectured Job on the very point Elihu is making!

Men of understanding (verse 10 NIV; NRSV, *you who have sense*) conveys the same sarcasm as in verse 2.

Verse 11 restates the traditional view of divine reward/punishment.

The concept of *justice* (verse 12) is seen in terms of helping the weak, punishing the wicked, and blessing the righteous (see 29:12-20).

All humanity is dependent upon God's *spirit*, or *breath*, for life (verse 14).

Verses 17-20: Proof of God's ultimate justice and impartiality is that the Almighty can punish even kings. Job stated this earlier (12:17-25), but added that such punishment is whimsical.

Midnight (verse 20) symbolized the darkest, and therefore most frightening, period of night. It was at midnight that the Lord smote the first-born in Egypt (Exodus 11:4-5).

Compare verse 21 with 31:4.

Verse 23 is Elihu's reply to Job's request for a court date with God.

Verse 28: The wicked are punished because they abused the poor (see 22:6-9).

The Hebrew in verses 29-30 is difficult, with varied translations. The sense is that God is beyond human speculation and control.

114

Condemnation of Job (34:31-37)

Elihu ends as he began. He insults Job. Because he returns again to this theme, we see that Elihu cannot resolve his rage against the sufferer.

As in the two preceding verses, the Hebrew text is difficult, making a precise translation impossible. Elihu appears to be condemning Job's reluctance to confess; the consequence will be God's requital of the sufferer on God's own terms.

Compare verse 34 with verses 2 and 10*a*. Elihu uses the terms here in a flattering manner. If Job's friends agree with what Elihu has said, then they will be men of understanding. Perhaps Elihu is worried that the three men have agreed with Job's blasphemies, and hence need to be coaxed back to the correct way of thinking.

Elihu returns in verse 36 to the theme of Job's alleged association with the wicked (verse 8).

Job's *rebellion* (verse 37) is refusing to admit that God's ways can be as easily understood—or agreed with—as Elihu maintains. *Claps his hands* denotes an act of derision (see also 27:23).

§ § § § § § §

The Message of Job 32–34

To experience salvation, we need a mediator between God and ourselves. As seen above in the commentary on 33:23-30, such a being not only speaks to God on our behalf, which is Job's view. This mediator also speaks to us on behalf of God. Just as God discovers us anew through the words of the mediator, so do we discover God and the divine mandates for our lives.

Salvation means making changes in our lives. To be forgiven does not mean sitting back and enjoying free grace. The experience of salvation comes with a price tag. It means hearing God's commands for doing things differently in our lives, and then carrying out those changes. *We hear the mediator's words to us in different ways.* Elihu suggests that such words may come to us through dreams or through suffering (33:14-22). Other avenues may be meditation, prayer, or Scripture reading. However, without one essential ingredient, all these methods leave things open to a subjective interpretation by the individual. A person must seek the counsel of other persons who have heard the mediator's voice.

We should be careful if we tell someone else "the way it is." Elihu comes off as an angry adolescent. Intervening in a situation where a person is behaving destructively requires sensitivity. To intervene with Elihu's spirit may accentuate destructiveness.

God does not need defending! This is a recurring message in Job, but it must be emphasized again in turning to Elihu. His address to Job's friends in chapter 34 stems from his perception that God has been insulted by their inability to silence the sufferer. But does the angry arrogance of an Elihu make God appear any better?

§ § § § § § §

Introduction to These Chapters

Elihu's earlier words, as seen in Part 13, were more or less introductory. They afforded us a glimpse into the heart of this angry, self-righteous man. They also afforded Elihu an opportunity to criticize Job and Job's friends.

In turning to his final two speeches (35:1–16; 36:1–37:24), Elihu appears to be purposely assuming the title, "God's lawyer." He seems conscious (35:14) of Job's long speech (chapters 29–31), which summarized the sufferer's case against God and challenged the Almighty to appear in court. Accordingly, he claims that he still has something to say *on God's behalf* (36:2). That something is his own summary speech, where he tries to state God's case in such a way that there can be no doubt of the Lord's vindication.

He believes he can seal victory by silencing Job. He employs a two-pronged strategy. First, he beats down Job by pounding him with assertions of God's overwhelming power and God's overwhelming detachment from human dependency (chapter 35). Having thus shown Job that he has no claim on God's attention, Elihu launches into the second strategic part (chapters 36–37). Here he painstakingly shows Job how God is the great teacher. Everything that happens in history and in nature has behind it some lesson God is trying to impart. The best Job can do is stop rebelling against God and start listening to what the Lord is saying.

In this defense of the deity, Elihu says little that is new. The theme of God's transcending otherness has been played before (4:17-21; 11:7-12), as has the concept of God causing suffering so that people may learn (5:17-18). The manner in which he preaches, though, is unique. He carefully examines things and forms convincing arguments. In chapters 36 and 37, for example, he exhaustively looks at nature, extracting specific lessons that God is imparting. Such a style reflects his self-perception: He indeed is the Lord's articulate attorney.

Compared to his earlier speeches, his addresses here exhibit less self-consciousness and more self-confidence. He is not apologizing for his entrance, nor is he needing to assert or explain his authority. Although the arrogance remains (see 36:2-4), it is greatly diminished. Elihu is gradually forgetting himself as he speaks, with the result being a final discourse that is not only powerful but also hauntingly beautiful.

In terms of critical considerations, the comments made in the introduction to Part 13 should be reviewed; these deal with questions of style and authorship. Other than that, the final two speeches present no major structural problems. The reader should simply be aware of verses where the Hebrew text is corrupt, thus making a clear reading impossible (see 35:9-15; 36:5, 14; 16-25, 30b).

Here is an outline of Job 35–37.

I. Elihu's Third Speech (35:1-16)
    A. Definition of Job's sin (35:1-4)
    B. God's independence from humanity (35:5-13)
    C. Condemnation of Job (35:14-16)
II. Elihu's Fourth Speech (36:1–37:24)
    A. Arrogant introduction (36:1-4)
    B. God teaches us through pain (36:5-25)
    C. God teaches us through nature (36:26–37:22)
    D. Concluding praise and warning (37:23-24)

Definition of Job's Sin (35:1-4)

Elihu begins his third speech by painting a picture of Job's dark character. In the fourth friend's eyes, Job is guilty of the sin of arrogance before God. Specifically, Job has done two things. He has claimed innocence (verse 2). He has also asserted that there is no profit in being righteous (verse 3). This assertion contradicts the basic belief of Jewish orthodoxy espoused by Elihu: The righteous will be rewarded, while the wicked will be punished.

Note that Elihu is also addressing Job's friends. In his eyes, they have failed to respond adequately to Job's sins. They, too, should take lessons from what Elihu is about to say.

God's Independence from Humanity (35:5-13)

The arrogant person assumes that what affects her or him also affects God. Just because Job is suffering, consequently, he believes he may cry out to God and God will hear.

Elihu states emphatically that this is not the case. God does not have to respond to anyone's cries. Thus, the best thing for Job to do is to humble himself before God by repenting, then keeping silent.

"God's lawyer" makes two points to that effect in this section. God overpowers humanity (verses 5-8), and God does not need to answer the cries of the wicked (verses 9-13).

Since God dwells in the *heavens* (verse 5), looking up reinforces the Almighty's distinction from humanity.

Compare verses 6-7 to 22:2-4. The stress is that God freely acts toward humanity, without being coerced in any way.

Virtue and sin affect humans, not God (verse 8).

Even wicked people, when they hurt, *cry out* to God, hoping in the Lord's deliverance (verse 9). If arrogant sinners could make such a proclamation of praise, then God may answer them.

The *night* (verse 10) is the most vulnerable time for a person (see 34:20). The experiencing of God's presence at such a time enables *songs* to be joyfully sung.

Compare verse 11 with 12:7.

Pride (verse 12 NRSV; NIV, *arrogance*) makes it impossible for sinners to profess the sentiments of verses 10-11. The result is that they make an empty cry, which God will not *answer*.

Condemnation of Job (35:14-16)

Elihu wants to make sure Job does not miss his point. In demanding a court date with God, the sufferer is like the arrogant sinners in verses 9-13. God does not hear their *empty* cry (verse 13), and God will not hear Job's *empty talk* (verse 16).

Note the total lack of compassion in verse 14. What can be worse than saying to a sufferer—regardless of whether or not the person is "wicked"—that God does not care?

The sense of verse 15 seems to be that God is being lenient with Job by not punishing him more severely.

Multiplies words (verse 16) is one of Elihu's favorite derogatory phrases. (See 34:37*b*)

Arrogant Introduction (36:1-4)

The overbearing nature of this introduction is purposeful. Elihu is calling attention to the importance of what he is about to say in this fourth and final speech. In a manner similar to Job (chapters 29-31), he will attempt an exhaustively brilliant concluding statement.

Verse 4*b* may be too arrogant even for Elihu. The *one* who is *perfect in knowledge* perhaps refers to God (see 37:16*b*).

God Teaches Us Through Pain (36:5-25)

The first point Elihu makes underlines his belief that behind the suffering is a divine lesson for the sufferer.

Holding this section together is his repeated use of *afflicted* and *affliction* (verses 6, 8, 15, 21). Such adversity enables the sufferer to hear the "instruction" of the Lord: He or she is *acting arrogantly* and should thus repent (verses 9-10).

Some have suggested—-based on the difficult Hebrew—that verse 5 conveys the sense that God, who is *mighty,* does not *despise* the "innocent". This follows the rest of the section, where Elihu affirms God's continued punishment of those who do not repent.

In verse 6 Elihu directly contradicts Job's assertion (chapter 21) that God lets the wicked prosper.

Bound in fetters (verse 8 NRSV; NIV *chains*) was a punishment of Hebrew kings who "did evil in the sight of the Lord." Such chastisement was inflicted by invading, victorious armies (see 2 Chronicles 33:11).

The poet may have in mind in verses 9-11 King Manasseh, who repented after being punished (see 2 Chronicles 33:1-2, 10-13).

Verse 14: *In shame* (NRSV) may also be translated *among the cult prostitutes* (NIV). The use here implies that the sinner dies prematurely, participating in such pagan excesses. Some ancient religions believed that by engaging in intercourse at a shrine (with a cult prostitute), a person may influence the gods. This practice was prohibited in Judaism (Deuteronomy 23:17).

Job's prosperity was God's way of encouraging him to behave righteously. *Rich food* (verse 16) was a sign of such prosperity (see 15:27).

The sense of verse 17 seems to be that Job has opinions about God's justice that are incorrect. One such belief is that the wicked get away with their sin (chapter 21).

Verse 21 is the moral of the preceding verses: Endure the *affliction* and turn away from challenging God, which is *iniquity* (NRSV; NIV, *evil*).

Verses 24-25: As in 33:26-28, Elihu (in comfort) exhorts Job to praise God during his affliction.

God Teaches Us Through Nature (36:26-37:22)

Having discerned the lesson God teaches in suffering, Elihu turns to seeking the divine admonitions in nature. Specifically, he searches the seasons looking for clues from God: fall (36:26-33), winter (37:1-13), and summer (37:14-22).

It should be mentioned that this categorizing is not exact. Elihu, rather, excerpts different qualities of these seasons and draws conclusions from them. He is regarding nature's mysteries with a sense of theological awe.

The characteristics of autumn display God's providential power. These include abundant *rain* (verses 27-29*a*), *thunder* and *lightning* (verses 29*b*-30, 32-33), and ripened crops (verse 31).

This translation of the difficult Hebrew in verse 30 makes little sense. Perhaps *roots of the sea* (NRSV; NIV depths . . .) signifying the depths of earth, are meant to contrast with the flashes of lightning high in the heavens. God reigns, whether at the pinnacle of the sky or at the bottom of the sea.

Lightning (verse 32) is the most dramatic display of God's supremacy (see Zechariah 9:14). Its flashes reveal one of God's lessons: The Almighty *is jealous with anger against iniquity* (33*b*, NRSV; see NIV footnote).

In turning to winter, Elihu continues his reflection on God's use of *thunder* and *lightning*. He then notes the other signs of this season. These are *snow* (verse 6), hibernation (verses 7-8), the *cold* (verse 9), and *ice* (verse 10). As in autumn, Elihu stresses that God providentially governs these forces.

The pounding of Elihu's *heart* (verse 1) demonstrates the excitement and awe he feels as he discovers God's ways in nature.

Verse 7 describes one of the lessons Elihu gleans from this season. God gives us the cold in order to make people stop working in the fields. In the warmth of their homes, they thus have an opportunity to reflect upon and worship the Lord.

Chamber and *driving winds* (verse 9) are poetic descriptions of the source of the chilling winter winds. The King James translation makes this clearer: *Out of the south cometh the whirlwind, and cold out of the north.* Compare this image to Ecclesiastes 1:6.

Note Elihu's earlier uses of the term *breath of God* (verse 10) in 32:8, 18; 33:4. The forces of nature, as well as people, are dependent upon the blowing of God's Spirit.

Verse 13 is another lesson Elihu discerns. The reasons behind God's absolute control over nature are to correct people, to help the *earth,* and to forgive people. Forgiveness is synonymous with *love* (see Numbers 14:18-19).

The key descriptions of summer are blistering heat (verse 17) and a blazing sun (verse 21). Note that Elihu's style changes in this section. Verses 15-18 contain a series of rhetorical questions, similar to the ones posed to Job in the whirlwind speeches (chapters 38-41). The questions are directed to Job and seem to ask, "You are beaten down by God's summer, and yet you would dare teach God anything?"

Balancings (verse 16, NRSV; NIV *poised*) refers to the suspension of clouds without visible support. This was a profound mystery to the ancient mind.

South wind (verse 17) refers to hot desert air, possibly from the arid Negeb region in southern Palestine.

Verse 18 refers to the belief that the sky was a mysterious, reflecting, solid *(hard)* mass. It separated the earth below from the heavens above, corresponding to the *firmament* (NIV, *expanse;* NRSV, *dome*) in Genesis 1:6-8.

Verse 19 is a sarcastic allusion to Job's desire to present his *case* before God (13:18).

The result of challenging God is total self-destruction (verse 20*b*).

The *north* (verse 22) is a poetic reference to the home of

God (see the commentary on 26:7). Gold (*golden splendor*) symbolized royal power.

Concluding Praise and Warning (37:23-24)

Just as Job succinctly summarized his case (31:35-37), so now does Elihu. His concluding argument in defense of God is simple: God is beyond us in every capacity, and our only proper response is fear. This has obvious similarities to the poem on wisdom in chapter 28; compare verse 23*a* to 28:13, 21; and verses 24*a* to 28:28.

§ § § § § § §

The Message of Job 35–37

These speeches raise two immediate questions. The answers to them show the deep rift between the orthodox Elihu and the suffering, exploring Job.

Does God control nature and history with a teaching hand? Elihu's response is an emphatic Yes! There is no doubt in his mind that everything that happens to people—from a chariot accident to an earthquake to a war—is carefully orchestrated by the teaching God. Suffering is thus easy to explain. God gives it to us purposely; we should patiently bear it, searching for the moral behind it.

Job is not so sure. He has questioned why things happen. His conclusion is that there can be no justifiable reason for many of the unfair happenings around him. He has accused God of insensitivity. He is on the verge of believing that God relates to creation in a manner different from the all-powerful, cut-and-dried view espoused by Elihu.

Does God operate within an air-tight legal system? Once again, Elihu answers with a strenuous affirmation. God holds the scales. If people do not toe the line precisely, they are punished severely. Even when sinners cry out for help, God turns a deaf ear; if they had first been penitent, they would have earned God's favor (35:9-13).

Job refuses to believe this. God cannot wear a blindfold while holding the scales. Human pain must take priority over impartial laws. A suffering creation must sway the Lord so as to bend those divine mandates. This is, after all, part of Job's reasoning behind doing something as fantastic as challenging God to court.

§ § § § § § §

PART FIFTEEN Job 38–39

Introduction to These Chapters

Then the LORD *answered Job out of the whirlwind* (38:1).
With this introduction, God steps into the drama. The
Lord will make two speeches, the first of which appears
in these chapters.

This divine appearance is both surprising and
humorous. Picture Job's righteous friends. Everything
they believe rules out such a phenomenon. For Elihu
especially (chapters 32–37), such an appearance is
incomprehensible. In his thinking, if God were to appear
to anyone, it should be to himself, the righteous one—not
to the blaspheming Job. But a whirling dust storm arises,
and out of it blasts the divine voice—directed to a man
covered with sores, wishing for death.

The utterances from the storm seem harsh at first.
Earlier, the sufferer had hurled invectives and challenges
at God. It is unthinkable, then, that placid words would
flow from the Lord's lips when the whirlwind finally
stirs. The rage of the exploding dust symbolizes the
turbulent feelings of the Almighty.

At the eye of the storm is the divine need to turn the
tables on Job. Job has dared to question God. Now it is
God's turn to question Job. The Lord's speech in chapters
38 and 39 is, for the most part, a series of rhetorical
inquiries. The subject is creation/nature. Where was Job
when God created the earth? And where is Job when God
cares for the beasts of the wilderness? Such questions are

not meant to be answered. They are meant to build in Job a healthy respect for the Lord.

It is a mistake, however, to let such abrasiveness overshadow the main point of the whirlwind: the healing of the fragmented, wounded relationship between Job and God. A lover cannot easily stay away from the beloved; if that happens, the love is not true. Similarly, God cannot stay away from this special person. The suffering and loneliness—of God as well as of Job— have been long enough. It is time to deal with the hurtful words and painful experiences. It is time to move on in their relationship—to a deeper, more intimate plateau.

In reading God's two addresses, one precaution must be observed. The reader should not look through the lenses of twentieth-century logic. If we were writing the book, then the Lord's speeches would deal with Job's earlier questions. We find, though, no such replies. Consequently, some reject chapters 38–41 (partially or totally) as not authentic.

Dismissal on such grounds does injustice to the poet's work. He thought in categories different from ours. He also wrote from a faith-centered, relationship-oriented perspective. It is important to remember that the purpose of the whirlwind speeches is to restore a relationship. They are not delivered by a professor. They are spoken by a lover.

Chapters 38 and 39 do not present any major critical problems. Certainly the customary impossible-to-interpret verses appear (see, for example, 38:36; 39:13b). These stem from corrupt texts or Hebrew words used so rarely as to make their meaning questionable

The major difficulties of these chapters, however, arise from the subject matter. They are packed with allusions to the natural world as seen through the eyes of an ancient Hebrew writer. The challenge to us is faithfully stepping into his sandals and experiencing creation as he did.

Here is an outline of these chapters.

God's Command to Job (38:1-3)

Job had longed for a confrontation with God. Now it is happening. But it is on the Lord's terms, not Job's. God does not reply to questions; the Almighty asks them.

This first speech begins with LORD, the intimate Hebrew word for the deity. The term originates in Exodus 4:13-15, and is also rendered *Yahweh* and *Jehovah*. This is in contrast to the rest of the poem, where the generic name is used (translated simply as *God*). This use denotes a change in the way God relates to Job. God is no longer an "object" for speculation. God is a "subject," the Lord who answers person-to-person.

Whirlwind (NRSV; NIV, *storm*) refers to a whirling desert dust storm. Such turbulences, or other unusual occurrences of nature, often accompanied divine appearances (see Psalm 18:6-15).

Who is this that darkens counsel (verse 2) carries the sense of, "Who confuses the understanding of my ways?"

Verse 3 is almost a playful challenge. *Gird up your loins* (NRSV) means *brace yourself* (NIV), as a soldier would before a battle. The onslaught will be with questions.

God's Control of Creation (38:4-15)

The point behind the Lord's barbed inquiries is to highlight human limitations by illustrating divine power. The area in which this is best seen is that of Creation. The Lord's speech explores three aspects of this: the creation of the land (verses 4-7); the containment of the seas (verses 8-11); the establishment of day and night (verses 12-15).

Like a master engineer, God measured the earth, built

supports for it, and suspended it in the midst of nothingness (verses 4-7). Compare this with the way God hung the clouds, mentioned in 37:16.

Morning stars (verse 7) and angels were heavenly witnesses of God's creative act. They looked down, saw the creation of the earth, and gave praise.

Verses 8-11: The *sea,* as viewed from its volatile clashes against land, was respected as a powerful—almost spiritual—force. When it was created—*burst forth from the womb*—God had to subdue it: with *doors, bars,* and a swaddling band (infants' clothes).

Looking across the sea toward the horizon, *clouds* (verse 9) appear to touch the water, restraining it.

As noted earlier in several places (24:13-17, 34:22, 36:20), each *dawn* (verse 12) protects the righteous from the covert deeds of the wicked. God's ordering its *place* in creation was thus a sign of the Creator's benevolent care.

When God commands the sun to rise, then all the *wicked*—who took cover under the *skirts* of darkness—will be seen clearly (*shaken out,* verse 13).

Clay takes on a clear impression when a seal is stamped upon it. The dawn has a similar effect upon the wicked. It clearly marks them so that *they stand forth* (verse 14; see the Revised Standard Version footnote). The *wicked,* thus detected by the dawn, are powerless.

God's Knowledge of Creation (38:16-38)

The natural world held countless wonders for the ancient Hebrews. The understanding of such things rested solely with God. This speech details many of these mysteries. The sheer number of them gives the impression that the Almighty's wisdom is inexhaustible:
- the depths of the sea and the earth (verses 16-18);
- the "home" of daylight and darkness (verses 19-21);
- the "home" of snow, hail, and storms (verses 22-24);
- the "home" of rain (verses 25-28);

• the "home" of ice (verses 29-30);
• the ordering of the heavens (verses 31-38).

Verses 16-18: The dead dwelt under the suspended earth, in Sheol (see the commentary on 7:9). The depths of the sea brought one close to its entrance (see 28:12-14, 20-22).

Declare (NRSV; NIV, *Tell me*) is a repeat of the Lord's challenge to Job in verse 3.

Day and night, as noted in verses 12-15, are separate powers controlled by Yahweh (see also Genesis 1:3-5). God stores them in their respective homes, calling each forth at the appropriate time.

Compare verse 21 to 15:7.

Which (verse 23) refers to hail, one of God's instruments of justice. (See Exodus 9:22-26; Isaiah 28:2; Haggai 2:17.)

The Hebrew word translated *light* (verse 24 NRSV; NIV, *lightening*) may also mean *wind,* coordinating it with the rest of the verse. *East wind* is a hot desert wind, another instrument of God's justice (see the commentary on 15:2).

Channel (verse 25; see 28:10) is a trench in the sky through which the rains may pour. The sky was believed to be solid (37:18), so such an avenue was necessary.

Verse 25b: See 28:26.

Verse 26 is a reference to God's caring for all creation. The Lord's kindness is not directed solely to humanity.

The freezing of water (verses 29-30) was not viewed as a natural occurrence; God called forth ice, replacing water with it.

The mysteries of the heavens are described in two parts: the stars (verses 31-33) and the meteorological phenomena (verses 34-38).

See the commentary on 9:9 regarding the constellations. *Mazzaroth* (NRSV; NIV; *constellations*) is a constellation of disputed location; this is its only reference in the Bible. *Chains* and *cords* poetically depict the ordering of the constellations, while *lead* and *guide* describe their movements across the sky.

The meaning of verse 36 is impossible to ascertain. It contains Hebrew words used only here, thus making translation difficult. For example, the word rendered *mists* has also been translated *heart* and *rooster*.

Wisdom (verse 37) here conveys the sense of knowing natural laws. This contrasts with the poet's use of it in 39:17, 26.

Verse 38 describes land saturated by rain.

God's Care for Creatures (38:39–39:30)

Just as the mysteries of creation are the province of God, so also are the mysterious ways earth's creatures are cared for. Only the Almighty could be so wise and powerful as to insure protection for all living things. Job wanes in comparison to such a mighty Lord.

In a style similar to that of the preceding section, several examples are given. Such a listing evokes a sense of awe at the extent of God's power: the lion (38:39-40); the raven (38:41); the mountain goat and deer (39:1-4); the wild ass (39:5-8); the wild ox (39:9-12); the ostrich (39:13-18); the horse (39:19-25); the hawk and eagle (39:26-30). Note that of these creatures, only the horse is domesticated. The others are outside human control; God alone masters them.

Compare verses 39-40 to Psalm 104:21-22.

Compare verse 41 to Psalm 147:9.

The *mountain goat* (39:1) is an ibex, a goat with long, backward-curving horns. It inhabits high and dangerous mountain regions (see Psalm 104:18). The *doe* is a red deer which, like the ibex, can travel with ease along ridges and cliffs (see Psalm 18:33). Since these animals were rarely seen, it was impossible to know their mating and birthing habits.

The *wild ass* (verse 5 NRSV; NIV, *wild donkey*) is an

onager, a wild, mule-like creature inhabiting wilderness areas far from cities (see Psalm 104:11).

Salt land (verse 6 NRSV; NIV, *salt flats*) refers to an arid, uninhabitable region (Psalm 107:34), the onager's refuge.

Similar in appearance to its domesticated cousin, the *wild ox* (verse 9) is untamable. It is so strong that it eludes captivity (see Psalm 22:12-13).

The Hebrew of verse 13 is difficult. The sense of this and the following verses is that the *ostrich* is a stupid, clumsy creature that endangers its own eggs (see Lamentations 4:3). The fact that the ostrich survives at all is a testimony to God's wise care.

Wisdom, as used here in verse 17, is synonymous with common sense.

Despite its stupidity, this land bird is faster than a *horse* (verse 18). *Rider* may refer to an ostrich hunter.

The poet's knowledge of and respect for the *horse* surfaces in verses 19-25. The image is that of a stallion eager for battle.

Wisdom (verse 26) here denotes the natural instincts of creatures. *Hawk* probably refers to the sparrow hawk, although there were several species in ancient Palestine. *South* refers to migration.

There were two types of eagles in biblical Palestine—the golden and the imperial. Note that the poet, as in his description of the wild goat and hind (verses 1-4), is impressed by the eagle's inhabiting high, inaccessible places (verses 27-30). Compare this with Jeremiah 49:16.

§ § § § § § §

The Message of Job 38–39

God is a person, not an idea. An idea does not speak from a whirlwind. An idea does not have a proper name. An idea cannot hold a conversation.

In reading the book of Job, it is easy to forget this. Given our intellectual bent, we look for philosophical solutions to suffering. Deducing trite formulas ("God gives us pain to teach us a lesson"), we ignore the real message of the biblical writer. The answer to the problem of pain is not found in an idea but in a person. That person is a Lord who confronts us with the very real possibility of a life-changing relationship.

A relationship with this person involves respect as well as intimacy. Sometimes, in a love relationship, one person takes the other for granted. That individual loses sight of the special nature of the beloved. At such a time, the blinded person must regain the feeling of awe, of respect, for the other.

This is Job's problem. His openness with God shows that he has little difficulty being intimate. What he needs, however, is to recover respect. God's speech is nothing less than an attempt to make him realize this. To take God for granted is death. To express all sorts of feelings to God, while respecting God's "otherness"—that is life.

Appreciation of creation leads to a greater respect for God. One of the curses of our modern mindset is the ease with which we lose our wonder of the world around us. Science and technology explain things away and give us tools for mastery. Genes and computer chips make us gods.

Such an attitude was not only unthinkable to the poet—it was idolatrous. The author of Job was in faithful, simple awe of the world we so easily dismiss. Everything seemed fresh and mysterious. Everything pointed to the greatness of God. It is little wonder that he chose this theme for the speech intended to instill respect in the irreverent Job.

Listening to these verses of praise penned by the poet may help call us back to our root relationship. Rekindling childlike awe of a God who carefully calls the sun to rise each day is essential. It is the beginning of appreciating the God who makes the sun rise on the unjust as well as the just. It is the beginning of respecting the God who sent Jesus.

§ § § § § § §

PART SIXTEEN Job 40–41

Introduction to These Chapters

The authenticity of this section, containing the Lord's second speech, has been questioned by some. One reason for this is the feeling that the second address is unnecessary. Job is silenced at the end of the Lord's first confrontation with him. Since the blasphemer is quieted, why should there be another speech?

This question misses the point. God's intent is not to force a strangled, silent submission. Rather, the Lord wants to renew a healthy, more intimate relationship. The first speech obviously does not do this (see Job's response in 40:4-5), so God tries again. The address found in these two chapters, thus, is vital.

At first glance, the strategy appears similar to that found in chapters 38-39. God makes forceful statements and asks questions to which Job cannot respond. It is as if God is trying to elicit a response of humiliation from the sufferer.

There is a subtle twist, though. The Lord focuses on two specific acts of Creation: the *Behemoth* (40:15-24) and the *Leviathan* (41:1-34). The description of the former pinpoints the awesome creative power of God. The description of the latter details God's powerful subduing of evil so that creation may truly be considered good.

Such scrutiny of the creative act produces a lasting effect. The final impression of the speech unmistakably paints God's portrait in positive, warm colors. Even with

135

suffering, the world around Job points to a God who painstakingly ensures that good will triumph.

Since these two creatures play such a vital role in the Lord's second speech, they should be examined. *Behemoth* has been most commonly identified as either an elephant or a hippopotamus. Such mammoth creatures inspired awe in the ancient world; they were signs pointing to the power of the Creator. In later Jewish literature (2 Esdras 6:49-52), Behemoth is depicted as a mythical monster, the land counterpart to Leviathan.

In Hebrew, *Leviathan* (also known as *Rahab*) suggests *coil*, as in the coils of a serpent. It has been identified as a crocodile. However, the term has mythological roots. According to ancient myths, Leviathan was a strong sea serpent, symbolic of evil and chaos. This monster had to be subdued by the creator-god in order for creation to prosper.

This myth was taken over by biblical writers to symbolize God's power. (See "How the Book Was Written" in the Introduction.) Psalm 74:12-14, for instance, refers to God crushing the Leviathan, described as a dragon with several heads. Such symbolism is important to the writer of Job. He has alluded throughout to the myth (3:8; 7:12; 9:13; 26:12-13). Now he uses it to conclude God's speech.

Focusing on such beasts appears to be a strange way of renewing the relationship with Job. It does not seem very personal. It should be noted, though, that such intimacy with God comes only within the context of "fear," or respect, of God. God the Creator, who makes colossal giants, suggests the Lord's otherness to Job. God the lover, who slays the dragon so that creation will survive, suggests the Lord's "for-ness" to Job. Taken together, Job comes into a new understanding—and appreciation—of God.

Other than the issues revolving around the question of authenticity, these chapters do not present major critical problems. The only thing that should be noted is the difference in chapter-verse designation between the Revised Standard Version and the Hebrew text. The designation of 41:1 in the RSV is actually 40:25 in the Hebrew. This commentary will follow the RSV.

Here is an outline of chapters 40-41.

I. God's Challenge to Job (40:1-2)
II. Job's Refusal to Answer (40:3-5)
III. God's Second Speech (40:6–41:34)
    A. God's command to Job (40:6-7)
    B. God's power over people (40:8-14)
    C. God's creation of Behemoth (40:15-24)
    D. God's defeat of Leviathan (41:1-34)

God's Challenge to Job (40:1-2)

Against the backdrop of questions posed to Job in the preceding two chapters, God now demands a response. Job has been talkative in challenging the Lord to a debate. God has answered. What will Job say?

Behind this is the question, "Can anyone really contend with God?" Some suggest an alternate rendering of the Hebrew which gives a translation more in keeping with the remainder of the verse: "Will the one who argues with God submit?"

Job's Refusal to Answer (40:3-5)

Job responds by acknowledging his smallness compared to God's greatness. However, he has already admitted as much (14:1-2; 16:7-8). By refusing to say any more than this, Job is refusing to submit. He will not say anything new. He will maintain an angry silence.

By putting his hand over his mouth (verse 4), Job is giving God a sign of absolute silence (see the similar images in 21:5b and 29:9b).

Verse 5 is a poetic way of saying, "I have already spoken, and I will not say any more." For other occurrences of this way of emphasizing something, see 5:19 and 33:14.

God's Command to Job (40:6-7)

Upon hearing Job's stubborn reply, God tries again. This introduction to the second whirlwind speech is basically the same as that of the first (see the commentary on 38:1, 3). Behind the serious tone is a playfulness. God does not need to converse with Job. The Lord could withdraw and let Job die a death of angry isolation. God, though, passionately begins another speech. Just as God does not give up on creation, neither will the Lord give up on someone as special as Job.

God's Power Over People (40:8-14)

With a directness lacking in the first speech, Job is asked quite bluntly if he can deal with people in a manner similar to God's. In these opening remarks, God challenges Job's earlier accusation that the Almighty is unjust in dealing with people. God humbles kings and exalts the powerless. Can Job do that?

The King James renders verse 8a, *Wilt thou also disannul my judgment righteousness?* God details the indirect accusation made in 38:2: Job is questioning the Almighty's sense of justice.

Verse 13 is a reference to death (*in the dust;* see 7:21) and to Sheol, the land of the dead.

Verse 14: By implication, Job cannot save himself. He is dependent upon God.

God's Creation of Behemoth (40:15-24)

The words of an admiring spectator ornament the description of this creature. Note that the rhetorical questions directed to Job, common to the rest of the whirlwind speeches, are absent. This section is simply a praise of the Creator by praising one of the Lord's most stupendous works. It is as if the poet, caught up in describing Behemoth, temporarily forgot the relevance of all this to Job: The angry blasphemer cannot confront such a powerful Creator.

The poet stresses that Behemoth, like Job, is God's creation. Also, God provides food (*grass*) for the beast, just as God provides for the sufferer.

Loins (verse 16) were viewed as the seat of a creature's strength.

Verse 19 reemphasizes God's creation and control over the powerful animal.

Verses 20-23, like 15*b*, depict God's careful nurturing of the beast. Even the mighty Behemoth is nothing unless the Lord provides for it.

Lotus (verse 21) may refer to the Egyptian water lily. It may also allude to a thorny shrub common in Palestine.

By implication, only God can subdue Behemoth.

God's Defeat of Leviathan (41:1-34)

The difficulty in reading this passage stems from mixing images regarding Leviathan. Viewing it sometimes as a crocodile and as a demonic dragon at other times may be confusing. It seems best, considering the elaborate description in verses 13-34, to view Leviathan solely as the mythological monster. The stress is upon describing Leviathan's terrifying appearance and strength. Mortals cannot easily approach such a monster. God, its creator, however, treats it as a plaything.

The rhetorical questions, indicative of the predominant style of the whirlwind speeches, return in the first seven verses of the section. The remainder of the chapter is penned in a manner similar to that of the Behemoth passages: an admiring description of the beast and a praise of the Creator.

Verses 1-2 describe the ancient method of capturing a crocodile. A baited hook was used, and strong *cords* (NRSV; NIV, *rope*) bound to the mouth. These verses suggest that though a fierce crocodile can be subdued in this manner, the ferocious Leviathan can never be captured.

The humorous questions in verses 3-8 ask Job, "Can you do anything you want with Leviathan, even making it your pet?" It is implied that God can toy with the monster.

A crocodile can be killed (verse 7). However, Leviathan's skin is doubly thick (verse 13), with its back like *rows of shields* (verse 15). Thus, *harpoons* and *spears* are useless against it.

Verses 9-11: This section is a philosophical aside. In case the point of the preceding verses is missed, it is bluntly stated here. Since God subdues the mighty Leviathan, it is ridiculous to think that a mere mortal can wrestle with God.

An exact rendering of verse 11 is impossible. The sense is that God is in debt to no one.

Verse 12, too, is difficult to translate. Taking it as it appears in the Revised Standard Version, God is proud of creating such a powerful creature. This serves as an introduction to the list of the beast's demonic features in verses 13-34.

Doors (verse 14) refer to weaknesses in the creature's skull through which it could be penetrated. Guarding such doors, however, are ominous *teeth*.

Leviathan's eyes resemble the bright sun peering over a dark horizon.

Wherever the monster goes, *terror* (verse 22 NRSV; NIV, *dismay*) is felt by all.

A *body* of flesh (verse 24) can be pierced. Leviathan's, however, is like a *millstone* and, *hence*, impregnable.

The *mighty* literally means *gods* (verse 25). In mythology, the gods were afraid of Leviathan. By contrast, God regards the monster as a toy.

Verse 26: This is due to Leviathan's metal-like covering, frightening teeth, and stone-hard heart (verses 13-17, 23-24).

The hard, smooth *slingstones* (verse 28) shatter when they crash into the monster's impenetrable skin.

Potsherds (verse 30) were sharp fragments of pottery; Job used them to scrape his sores (2:8). A *threshing sledge* was a heavy weight, pulled by a horse, that rolled over grain. Leviathan rolls over anything in front of it, leaving destruction in its wake.

The boiling deep (verse 31) refers to the churning of water produced by the serpent. To make a *pot of ointment,* materials were sliced, crushed, and violently stirred. Leviathan has this effect on the sea.

When the monster is aroused, the sea turns white with foam, like one with white hair (v. 32).

Verse 33 summarizes the poet's point. The beast is the archenemy, a seemingly supernatural foe. God's power over it causes humans to burst forth in praise.

Because nothing on earth can defeat it, Leviathan is the epitome of arrogance, doing whatever it wants. All other proud creatures (verse 34) pale in comparison to it.

§ § § § § § §

The Message of Job 40–41

The hurting person is part of the Lord's creation. Early in the speech God subtly reminds Job that he is a creature, not a god; *Behold Behemoth, which I made as I made you* (40:15*a*). Challenging God could place Job above the created order. Such a position sets him up for self-salvation and isolation. The first thing God must do is remind Job of his proper place in the scheme of things.

God the Creator is trustworthy. Job had argued against God's sense of justice. To him, human affairs appeared to be a matter of chance, without any just, benevolent, guiding hand. God directly confronts this.

Such news is gospel for sufferers. Loneliness and bewilderment accompany pain. To whom can we turn? In whom can we trust? It can only be someone who has been proven worthy. The account of the defeat of pain, of the defeat of the Leviathan in our lives, points to God.

God the Creator deals with a hurting creation in personal ways. In the final analysis, the most important thing about the whirlwind speeches is the whirlwind. The content, though helpful, is not as essential as God's active presence. The Lord freely engages Job, one on one. There are no angels or other intermediaries. God and the sufferer meet face to face. As the Lord met Leviathan to subdue him, so does the Lord meet Job, to heal him.

The hope of the sufferer is that in the midst of hurt a whirlwind will arise. Job discovered a God who answered him, personally, in the roar of a storm. We, too, can be confident that the Lord will personally, specially, talk to us when we face a dark world. From the mighty whirlwind we will perhaps hear God's warm, clear voice.

§ § § § § § §

PART SEVENTEEN Job 42

Introduction to This Chapter

The action prior to this chapter highlighted the Lord's passionate attempts to restore a relationship with Job. The two preceding chapters contain the second whirlwind speech, which detailed God's creative power and benevolent care (see Part 16).

The question opening this chapter is thus, What will Job do? His previous response was in short, clipped, angry sentences (40:3-5). Will this one be any different? Will the Lord's second speech produce better results?

The opening verses of chapter 42 answer this. Job admits to rashness. He confesses that he spoke without really knowing all the facts. He praises God. And he concludes his speech promising humility: . . . *Therefore I despise myself, and repent in dust and ashes* (verse 6).

This response must be placed in perspective. The friends had relentlessly dogged Job, trying to beat him into submission. Their only reward was frustration. Now God speaks. In only a fraction of the length of the friends' speeches, the Lord echoes their basic sentiments (that is, divine power and justice). Then Job repents.

Why does God do what the friends couldn't? Because the Lord speaks to Job's feelings, not his thoughts. Without coercion (who can coerce God?), and with no ulterior motive, the Almighty personally appears and passionately speaks. Job is moved. He admits that this was what drew him to repent: *I had heard of you by the hearing of the ear, but now my eye sees you* (verse 5 NRSV).

Job sees God reaching out, trying to ease his suffering and restore a love relationship. Behind the Lord's words are the whisperings of a lover. His reply is but a passionate praise to that lover.

The remainder of chapter 42 consists of the prose epilogue. As noted in the Introduction (see "How the Book Was Written"), this is the conclusion of the tale appropriated by the poet.

In this ending, two very important things happen. First, God criticizes Job's friends, commanding them to beseech Job's intercession (verses 7-9). Following this, the Lord restores Job's fortunes (verses 10-17).

These events show that the conclusion of the book is not just a happy one. It is also a surprising, turning-the-tables one. Throughout, the book has portrayed the friends as the righteous ones. They had health and wealth. They talked about God in terms of statements, not questions. Job, on the other hand, was the complete opposite. The loss of his comfort and well-being seemingly pointed to the shambles of his spiritual life. His speech was filled with angry oaths against God. Yet, in the end, this man was justified by the Lord, and the others chastised. Why?

It is a tribute to the genius of the author that he concludes the book by dramatically answering the question that began it. The friends epitomize the smug theology of ancient Israel: God blesses the righteous and punishes the wicked. Job, conversely, symbolizes the person who is honest with herself or himself, and who seeks new ways of relating to the Lord. Who is right? The book's conclusion givers the author's answer. The one who asks questions, seeking and struggling through a passionate faith, is the one the Lord blesses.

In terms of critical considerations, the biggest question is the reappearance of the prose portion. If it were tied to

144

the ending of the prose introduction (2:13), then—filling in the blanks—the original story may have appeared as follows: Job's friends, agreeing with his wife, urged the sufferer to *curse God and die* (2:9). Job patiently persevered, however. Consequently, the sufferer was blessed.

It is no accident, though, that the poet adds this to the conclusion of his poem. Following as it does the extensive dialogues, it makes a different and powerful statement. As seen above, and as will be seen in the commentary, this prose ending is the distinctive signature of the poet.

Here is an outline of Job 42.

I. Job's Response to God's Second Speech (42:1-6)
II. Prose Epilogue (42:7-17)
    A. God's Rebuke of Job's friends (42:7-9)
    B. God's Restoration of Job's fortune (42:10-17)

Job's Response to God's Second Speech (42:1-6)

Compare this to his first response, in 40:3-5. There Job was sullen. His gaze was inward, focusing on his hurt; *I* appears six times in that two-verse speech. Job was impervious to God's attempts for reconciliation. As a lover who has been hurt by the beloved, Job nursed his anger and was fearful of letting it go.

He has totally changed in the second speech. God's passionate overtures finally seduce him. His response is filled with humility. More importantly, though, it brims with praises to God. Job is looking past his hurt and seeing a loving Lord. The warm feelings he once had are rekindled. Regardless of what happens to him, he will love the Lord.

Job begins his response with praise. He acknowledges, finally, what God has said in the two speeches. By such an acknowledgment, Job is saying that God is just after all. This is not, though, an affirmation of the friends' simplistic formula of God punishing the wicked and rewarding the good. Job is simply affirming God's goodness, regardless.

Verse 3 repeats 38:2 (see the commentary on that verse.) Repeating God's words is an affirmation of God, as evidenced in the remainder of the verse. It is perhaps possible, also, to see in such repetition Job's subconscious reflection upon God's indictment of him.

What Job *did not understand* was the nature of God. Because of his suffering, God appeared callous and even evil. But now, because of the Lord's appearing in the whirlwind, Job sees *wonderful* things. At the apex is the realization that God is loving and just after all.

The first part of verse 4 is an attention getter, pointing to the importance of what follows (see 33:31). The rest of the verse repeats 38:3. In repeating this, Job affirms God's supremacy. God does not submit to questioning; God asks the questions.

Everything about God was speculation for Job. He only knew God *by the hearing of the ear* (verse 5). The Lord's appearance in the whirlwind, however, changes this: *but now my eye sees you.* This personal encounter alters the emotions as well as the intellect.

Job *despises* himself for having thought God was uncaring and unjust. The *ashes* in which he repents may be from his earlier acts of purification (see the commentary on 2:8).

God's Rebuke of Job's Friends (42:7-9)

These verses begin the prose epilogue. Only the three original friends are mentioned here; Elihu, the fourth friend who spoke in chapters 32-37, is omitted. It appears as if the companions have already left Job, since they are directed to go to him. Perhaps they departed out of frustration and disgust.

God addresses Eliphaz, since he is the oldest. The Lord's condemnation—*you have not spoken of me what is right* (verse 7)—is the poet's condemnation of the traditional theology espoused by the friends. The companions had twisted their perception of things in order to defend God. They had said, for example, that the wicked are punished; if they had been true to their senses, though, they would have observed that sometimes sinners prosper. The poet harshly criticizes such blindness. (See also the commentary on 13:7-11.)

The size of the burnt offering mentioned in verse 8 is huge. Numbers 23 and Ezekiel 45:21-25 mention offerings of similar size, but they were given on behalf of entire nations. The immensity of the sacrifice indicates the gravity of the friends' sin.

Regarding Job's intercessory power (verse 9), see Ezekiel 14:14, 20. Even such a gigantic offering is not enough. The friends need Job's prayer in order for God to accept it.

God's Restoration of Job's Fortune (42:10-17)

This concluding section is the "happy ending" of the book. God brings fullness to Job in all aspects of his life: in society (verse 11), in possessions (verse 12), and in his family (verses 13-15). In addition, the Lord allows Job to live a long time, so as to enjoy this prosperity (verses 16-17).

Note that only after Job prays for the friends does God reward Job with twice as much. The friends were not compassionate. They were rebuked by God. But when Job forgives them and prays for them, God restores his fortunes.

The fact that Job's brothers, sisters, and friends had abandoned him underlines the social implications of the doctrine of divine reward and punishment: Stay away from a sufferer, since that person is a sinner experiencing God's wrath. Note, though, that when they return, they comfort Job for all the *troubles* that *the* LORD *had brought upon him*. They have changed. They abandon the belief of divine reward and punishment. They acknowledge that

Job's suffering was a mystery, somehow centered in God. Their faith has deepened as a result of Job's struggles.

The *piece of money* (NRSV; NIV, *silver*) is a *qesitah,* a small weight of silver. Other Old Testament references (Genesis 33:19; Joshua 24:32) mention one hundred qesitahs being the price of a field. A *gold ring* was a valuable piece of jewelry in the ancient world, worn either in the nose (Genesis 24:47) or ear (Genesis 35:4). The money and jewelry are gifts welcoming Job back into the community.

Job's possessions have exactly doubled. Compare his new fortune with his original one, in 1:3.

Job now has the same number and ratio of children that he had in the beginning of the book (see 1:2). *Jemimah* means *dove* or *turtledove. Keziah* may be translated *cinnamon. Kerenhappuch* means *eyeshadow.* These names are symbols of female beauty. Cinnamon may refer to the spice in a perfume, while eyeshadow refers to the cosmetic. Job's daughters, with their beauty and wealth, would be secure in the world.

Of special note is that the daughters, not the sons, are named. Also, the women are given an inheritance along with their brothers, an amazing occurrence in the ancient male-dominated society.

Seeing four generations was extraordinary (see Genesis 50:23). This is another sign of God's blessing.

Verse 17: This is a traditional designation of honor for respected leaders in Jewish history (see Genesis 25:8). Considering what Job had gone through, he certainly deserved it!

§ § § § § § §

The Message of Job 42

The Lord never gives up. The fact that Job moves from cursing to praising shows this. God relentlessly pursues Job. The Lord visits him in a whirlwind. God puts together an elaborate speech. When that fails, the Lord constructs another. Finally, the ice in Job's heart melts. Overwhelmed by the Almighty's persistence, he returns the Lord's love.

Suffering produces an emptiness of the heart. The person in pain has little ability to open up to the world. Like Job in his first response to God, the sufferer turns inward. Such a person needs someone to intervene, to give a vision of hope, to love. God in the whirlwind is such a person. Our greatest challenge in helping a sufferer is to reflect that aggressive love. Our greatest challenge as a sufferer is to accept it.

God is the lover who vindicates the beloved. The restoration of Job's fortunes testifies to the worthiness of his life. This comes in the light of his friends' savage attempts to find evil and guilt in him. Because he holds fast to his integrity, he is not abandoned to an angry, lonely death. God says, by making the restoration, that the reward of such integrity is happiness. There is no sad ending.

It is too simplistic to say that the Lord will bless the sufferer. It is more to the point to say that as the sufferer struggles, calling out to God, then that person eventually discovers a new dimension. Job's integrity pushed him to a greater honesty with himself and with God. It allowed him an opportunity for a new exploration of faith. Our integrity, likewise, prepares us for a new life. That life comes from God, who vindicates our pain with a passionate love.

The new life discovered in suffering is nothing less than the kingdom of God. The closing verses of the book are deceptive. In listing Job's new fortune, they mention two radical things. Job's family and friends discover a new faith in God, and the daughters born to him are accorded equality with men. Such events point to more than a happy ending. They point to this realization: Wherever the sufferer encounters God, life will never be the same again. It will take on earthshaking proportions.

Perhaps this is the last—and best—word Job gives to the sufferer. In the enduring of pain, with honesty and with questioning, the sufferer catches a glimpse of the Kingdom. Words like faith, forgiveness, justice, and hope are no longer well-worn cliches. They are life-changing realities. Even if the suffering leads to death, the new life is still affirmed. That is because God—from the whirlwind of our lives—will never stop confronting us until we say, with Job, *I had heard of thee by the hearing of the ear, but now my eye sees thee* (42:5).

§ § § § § § §

Glossary of Terms

Abaddon: Another name for Sheol, the land of the dead.

Barachel: Father of Elihu; his name means *God has blessed.*

Bars of Sheol: A poetic designation of the doors, or entrance, to the abode of the dead.

Bear: A constellation of stars containing either the Big Dipper ("Great Bear") or Little Dipper ("Little Bear").

Behemoth: Commonly identified as either an elephant or hippopotamus. It also has mythological roots, believed to have been the land counterpart of Leviathan, the sea serpent.

Bildad: One of Job's friends, also known as the Shuhite. His name means either *God has loved* or *son of Hadad.*

Booth: A small, temporary, flimsy construction used by a watchman while on duty.

Breath of the Almighty: Another term for *Spirit*; all living creatures are dependent upon God's breath.

Broom Tree: A desert bush burned for warmth by wandering outcasts.

Buz: A tribe or territory, of uncertain location, in the Arabian peninsula; Barachel's homeland.

Buzite: The designation of someone from the tribe or territory of Buz.

Byword: A name or phrase used as a source of derision and ridicule.

Chaldeans: Inhabitants of a rugged region in southern Babylonia, a country north of Uz. Eventually Chaldea became synonymous with Babylonia.

Chambers of the South: A group of stars whose location is undertain.

Clap one's hands: A way of expressing disgust.

Doctrine of divine reward/punishment: The orthodox Jewish view, argued by Job's friends, that God rewards the righteous and punishes the wicked. Such a concept explains suffering as the consequence of God's chastisement.

East: A designation for countries east of Palestine, including Uz. It was an area known for its scholars.

East Wind: A hot desert wind, or *sirocco*, that destroys vegetation.

Elihu: The name of Job's fourth friend, appearing in Chapters 32–37; the son of Barachel, his name means *my God is he*.

Eliphaz: The oldest of Job's friends. From the town of Tema, his name possibly means *God is fine gold*.

Ethiopia: A territory south of Egypt, noted for gems such as topaz.

Fat: A sign of prosperity.

Fear of God: Respecting God's power and acknowledging total dependence upon the Almighty. This phrase designated the proper attitude one should have toward God.

Fire of God: A brush fire or lightning, viewed as a sign of God's displeasure or punishment.

Fool: A term used in Wisdom Literature (see the Introduction, "How the Book Was Written"), such as Proverbs, denoting one who does not display proper *fear of God*.

Freshets: Temporary streams of water resulting from melting snow or ice.

Heart: The center of the intellect in Hebrew thought; synonymous with *conscience*.

Heaven(s): The region above the earth, separated from it by the sky.

Hireling: A contracted and compensated worker leading a life of strenuous labor.

Holy ones: Another name for angels.

Jemimah: One of the three daughters born to Job when the Lord restored his fortunes; her name means *dove* or *turtledove*.

Job: The "hero" of the book, living in Uz; the name may mean *one who is at war with God*, *one born to be persecuted*, or *the repentant one*.

Justice: Viewed in terms of helping the weak, punishing the wicked, and blessing the righteous.

Kerenhappuch: One of the three daughters born to Job when the Lord restored his fortunes; her name means *eyeshadow*.

Keziah: One of the three daughters born to Job when the Lord restored his fortunes; her name means *cinnamon*.

Leviathan: A sea monster which, in mythology, had to be subdued by a god in order for creation to prosper; its name suggests *coil*, as in the coils of a serpent. Also known as *Rahab*.

Lord: An intimate Hebrew term for God, stemming from Exodus 4:14. Also translated as *Yahweh*.

Lotus: An Egyptian water lily, or a thorny Palestinian shrub.

Lyre: A harp-like instrument used in worship to praise God.

Mallow: A tasteless, soft plant grown in the wilderness and eaten by the poor.

Mazzaroth: A constellation of stars, of uncertain location.

Mediator: One who acts as an impartial go-between for two conflicting parties.

Millstone: A hard, heavy stone used for grinding grain.

Morning Stars: Bright stars visible at dawn, announcing the arrival of the sun. The brightest of these is Venus.

Na'ameh: A region in northwest Arabia, home of Zophar.

Naamathite: A resident of Na'ameh.

Nettle: A type of thorny bush or large, prickly weed.

Ophir: An ancient land of uncertain location, noted for the quality and abundance of its gold.

Orion: A constellation of stars representing the famous hunter in Greek mythology.

Orphans: A segment of Jewish society which was vulnerable to abuse by the wicked.

Papyrus: Fragile plants, grown in the Nile, easily destroyed.

Pipe: A flute-like instrument used in worship to praise God.

Pit: A descriptive term for the grave, commonly used in the Psalms.

Pledge: A promise that ensures a person's safety and/or prosperity.

Pleiades: A cluster of stars located in the constellation Taurus.

Poor: The easy target of the wicked, open to exploitation and abuse.

Potsherds: Sharp fragments of broken pottery, used for cutting and scraping.

Purslane: A small, weed-like plant containing bland juice and used in salads.

Qesitah: A small weight of silver, used as a form of currency.

Rahab: Another name for the sea monster *Leviathan*.

Ram: The name of the clan to which Elihu belonged.

Ransom: That which is given to someone so that a sin may be forgiven, or covered up.

Redeemer: A vindicator; one who avenges a person who has been wronged; one who administers justice on behalf of the weak.

Sabeans: Inhabitants of a region in the southern Arabian peninsula, sometimes called *Sheba*; it was located south of Uz.

Salt land: An arid region inhabited only by wild, sturdy creatures.

Satan: The *adversary*, or opponent, who challenges God regarding Job's character. One of the sons of God, Satan is an argumentative figure in the book, and not necessarily evil.

Shades: The dead who inhabit Sheol.

Sheba: Another name for the home of the Sabaeans, located in southern Arabia.

Sheol: The subterranean realm of the dead in Hebrew thought. Viewed as a simple resting place for the *shades*, it should not be confused with the New Testament concept of Hell.

Shuah: Bildad's tribe, which settled in the northeastern part of the Arabian peninsula.

Shuhite: A member of the tribe of Shuah.

Skiffs: Shallow, lightweight boats.

Sky: Believed to be a hard, mirror-like substance separating earth from the heavens.

Sons of God: An ancient term for divine beings, such as gods or angels.

Spirit: Two meanings in Job: (1) a night vision or ghost (4:15); and (2) the "wind" that comes from the Breath of God (32:8).

Tema: A town in the northern Arabian peninsula known for its commerce; the residence of Eliphaz.

Temanite: An inhabitant of the city of Tema.

Terrors: A term used in Job to designate the punishment of the wicked; it means *those things which wear down and destroy.*

Threshing sledge: A heavy weight, pulled by a horse, that rolled over grain.

Torrent bed: A swift, dangerous stream with a strong current.

Umpire: A powerful judge arbitrating between two disputing parties.

Uz: The homeland of Job, an area east of Palestine and located in the Syrian desert; possibly the ancient name for Edom.

Vault of heaven: Corresponding to *sky*, this separated earth from heaven.

Watchman: One who stands guard, protecting a person and/or property.

Weaver's shuttle: The part of a loom that passes rapidly back and forth, weaving yarn into cloth.

Whirlwind: A whirling desert dust storm, often accompanying divine appearances.

Wicked: A designation of those who have no fear of God and, consequently, mistreat the powerless.

Widows: A segment of Hebrew society who, because of the lack of male protection, were vulnerable to exploitation and abuse by the wicked.

Wisdom: Refers, in varying contexts, to: common sense; a knowledge of the mysterious workings of God and nature; the instincts of animals and other parts of the created order.

Yahweh: A Hebrew term for God, indicative of the intimate, covenantal nature of the Lord. Its origins are in Exodus 4:14.

Zophar: One of Job's friends, from Na'ameh. His name possibly means *singing bird.*

Guide to Pronunciation

Abaddon: AB-ah-don
Barachel: Bah-rah-KELL
Behemoth: Beh-HEE-moth
Bildad: BILL-dad
Buzite: BOO-zite
Chaldeans: Kal-DEE-ans
Elihu: Ee-HIE-hew
Eliphaz: EHL-ih-faz
Ethiopia: Ee-thee-OH-pia
Freshets: FRESH-ets
Hireling: HIRE-ling
Jemimah: Jeh-MY-mah
Job: JOHB
Kerenhappuch: Keh-ren-HAH-puk
Keziah: Keh-ZIGH-ah
Leviathan: Leh-VIGH-ah-than
Lyre: LIER
Mazzaroth: Mah-zah-ROTHE
Naameh: Nah-ah-MEH
Naamathite: Nah-ah-MAH-thite
Ophir: OH-fear
Orion: Oh-RYE-un
Papyrus: Puh-PIE-russ
Pleiades: PLEE-ah-deez
Purslane: PURS-lin
Qesitah: Keh-SEE-tah

Rahab: RAY-hab
Ram: RAHM
Sabeans: Sah-BEE-ans
Satan: SAY-tan
Sheba: SHEE-bah
Sheol: SHEE-ohl
Shuah: SHOO-ah
Shuhite: SHOO-hite
Tema: TAY-mah
Temanite: TAY-man-ite
Uz: UHZ
Yahweh: YAH-weh
Zophar: ZOH-far